The General Strike of 1926 in support of the miners was the most important dispute in British industrial history. It is the only occasion on which the vast majority of the working class have given their industrial, financial and moral support to a group of workers for more than one day.

This book examines the reasons for the dispute and its significance for British society. It focuses on the unfolding of events such as 'Black Friday', 'Red Friday' and the action of the rank and file, as well as the reaction of the Conservative Government and the constitutional issues raised. The author argues that the General Strike was almost inevitable, given the conflicting demands of the TUC and the Government. He also asserts that it was not the unmitigated disaster that it is often presented as being.

Apart from an original and accessible analysis of the General Strike, Keith Laybourn provides a lucid survey of existing historiography on the dispute and a useful section of key documents. His study offers an ideal update on a topic which has not seen a major textbook in seventeen years.

Keith Laybourn is Professor in History at the University of Huddersfield.

NEW FRONTIERS IN HISTORY
series editors
Mark Greengrass
Department of History, Sheffield University
John Stevenson
Worcester College, Oxford

The important new series reflects the substantial expansion that has occurred in the scope of history syllabuses. As new subject areas have emerged and syllabuses have come to focus more upon methods of historical enquiry and knowledge of source materials, a growing need has arisen for correspondingly broad-ranging textbooks.

New Frontiers in History provides up-to-date overviews of key topics in British, European and world history, together with accompanying source material and appendices. Authors focus upon subjects where revisionist work is being undertaken, providing a fresh viewpoint which will be welcomed by student and sixth formers. The series also explores established topics which have attracted much conflicting analysis and require a synthesis of the state of the debate.

Already published
C. J. Bartlett   Defence and diplomacy: Britain and the great powers, 1815–1914

Forthcoming titles
Michael Braddick   The nerves of state: taxation and the financing of the English state, 1558–1714
Ciaran Brady   The unplanned conquest: social changes and political conflict in sixteenth-century Ireland
David Brooks   The age of upheaval: Edwardian politics, 1899–1914
Conan Fischer   The rise of the Nazis
Mark Greengrass   Points of resistance in sixteenth-century Europe
Tony Kushner   The holocaust and its aftermath
Alan O'Day   Irish home rule
Panikos Panayi   Immigrants, minorities and British society, 1840–1919
Daniel Szechi   The Jacobites, Britain and Europe, 1688–1788

The
General Strike
of 1926

Keith Laybourn

Manchester University Press
Manchester and New York
Distributed exclusively in the USA and Canada by St Martin's Press

Copyright © Keith Laybourn 1993

Published by Manchester University Press
Oxford Road, Manchester M13 9PL, UK
and Room 400, 175 Fifth Avenue, New York, NY 10010, USA

Distributed exclusively in the USA and CANADA
by St Martin's Press, Inc., 175 Fifth Avenue, New York, NY 10010, USA

British Library Cataloguing-in-Publication Data
A catalogue record for this book is available from the British Library

Library of Congress Cataloging-in-Publication Data

Laybourn, Keith.
    The general strike of 1926 / Keith Laybourn.
       p.   cm. — (New frontiers in history)
    ISBN 0–7190–3864–2 (cloth). — ISBN 0–7190–3865–0 (pbk.)
    1. General Strike. Great Britain, 1926.   I. Title.   II. Series.
HD5365.A6L39   1994
331.89'25'094109042—dc20   93–28180
                                                 CIP

ISBN 0 7190 3864 2 *hardback*
       0 7190 3865 0 *paperback*

Photoset in Linotron Palatino
by Northern Phototypesetting Co Ltd., Bolton

Printed in Great Britain
by Bell & Bain Ltd, Glasgow

Contents

Acknowledgements *page* vii

List of abbreviations ix

Introduction 1

1 **Not 'out of a clear sky': the long-term causes of the General Strike** 9
   Interpretations 9
   Government, the employers, the coal industry and the TUC 1918–1925 13
   The wool and worsted textile dispute, 1925 22
   Conclusion 24

2 **The 1925 Coal Crisis and the nine-month respite** 27
   Red Friday, 31 July 1925 28
   The nine-month interregnum 31
   The Samuel Commission 36
   Negotiations 38
   The final efforts at settlement 40
   Conclusion 45

3 **'The wonderful response and the organisation we had': the Nine Days** 49
   The General Council and its conduct of the dispute 50
   The Government: objectives and preparations 54
   The General Strike at local level: organisation and administration 58

Contents

The General Strike at Bradford   63
Rank and file response   66
The effectiveness of the local authorities   67
Policing and violence   69
Communist influence   72
Conclusion   73

4 The Settlement   78
A constitutional strike   79
The Samuel intervention   81
The end of the strike   85
Conclusion   87

5 The return to work and the problem of the coal lock-out   89
Local reaction   90
The coal mining lock-out, April–November 1926   95
Conclusion   97

6 The consequences of the General Strike:
a watershed in British industrial relations?   100
The reckoning   104
The Trades Dispute Act, 1927   106
The consequences of the General Strike   108
Conclusion   115

Conclusion   118
Selected documents   122
Bibliographical Essay   154
Index   157

Acknowledgements

There are many individuals to whom I owe thanks for their help in the preparation of this book. The librarians and archivists of West Yorkshire, particularly, have given generously of their time and I would especially like to express my thanks to David James of Bradford Archives who allowed me access to the general strike material which is deposited in the West Yorkshire District Archives, Bradford branch. He also provided the photograph of the executive committee of the Bradford Council of Action which appears on the front cover. In addition, I must thank the Archive Division of the British Library of Political and Economic Science, at the London School of Economics, who allowed me to consult the Citrine and Lansbury paper. I also used the Henry Duckworth account of the 'Dover Dockers', which was deposited, as part of the Beveridge Collection, by Philip Mair, Beveridge's stepson, in the 1970s. Philip Mair died in the late 1980s and it has proved impossible to find out where copyright resides. The TUC also gave me permission to quote from their extensive collection of manuscripts and published material, and Crown Copyright material is published by permission of the Controller of Her Majesty's Stationery Office. Permissions were also obtained from Random House, UK. The Labour Research Department have given permission to reproduce the extracts from *Trades Councils in Action 1926*, which was undertaken by Emile Burns for the Labour Research Department. The author and the publisher also wish to apologise for any inadvertent infringement of copyright and have sought to keep within the publishers' convention in the use of some recently published secondary sources. In every case, the documents have been fully attributed. Every effort has been made to trace the copyright owner but anyone claiming copyright should get in touch with the author.

List of abbreviations

CPGB	Communist Party of Great Britain
FBI	Federation of British Industries
GWR	Great Western Railway
LMSR	London, Midland and Scottish Railroad
LNER	London and North Eastern Railway
MFGB	Miners' Federation of Great Britain
NCEO	National Conference of Employers' Organisations
NTW	National Transport Workers' Federation
NUR	National Union of Railwaymen
NUWM	National Unemployed Workers' Movement
OMS	Organisation for the Maintenance of Supplies
SIC	Special Industrial Committee (of the General Council)
SR	Southern Railway
TGWU	Transport and General Workers' Union
TUC	Trades Union Congress

Dedicated to my father,
Donald Laybourn (1924–1989),
who spent 43 years in the
Barnsley coal mines.

Introduction

The national strike, or the 'general strike' as it was termed by the press, commenced on the 3rd May, 1926 and lasted only nine days. It never was a general strike as the General Council did not call out all the members of the unions by any means. Indeed, they took steps to ensure that some employed in the basic industries stayed at work.
W. Citrine, 'Mining Crisis and the National Strike'.[1]

The General Strike, in support of the miners, which lasted for nine days from one minute to midnight on the 3 May until noon on the 12 May 1926, was the most important industrial conflict in British history. It is the only occasion on which the vast majority of the organised working class have given their industrial, financial and moral support to a group of workers for more than a day, although, as Citrine notes, not all the workers were called out. Indeed, it is the only occasion on which there has been a substantial national strike in support of any group of industrial workers in Britain. No event has ever divided the nation so sharply along class lines or produced so much bitterness; Arthur Scargill certainly captured the sentiment of many mining communities when he suggested that the miners' national strike of 1972 was revenge for 1926. Inevitably, the General Strike has attracted immense interest and attention from all sections of the political spectrum, all of whom have used it for their own ends.

When the dispute occurred between one and a half and one and three-quarter million workers, mainly those in vital

1

industries such as transport, electricity, building and gas, came out of work. This was in support of the one million miners who had been locked out on 30 April for refusing to accept lower wages once the subsidy to the coal industry which had been agreed on 31 July 1925, 'Red Friday', ran out. The decision to support the miners had been taken by the TUC at a meeting at Memorial Hall London, on 1 May and had received the over-whelming support of the movement. The TUC also gave power to its negotiating committee to deal with any arrangements which would settle the General Strike and lead to the re-opening of negotiations between miners and mine owners and prevent both wage reductions and an increase in hours in mining. Indeed, Ernest Bevin implored all those present 'in the name of the General Council, on every man and woman . . . to fight for the soul of labour and the salvation of the miners'.[2] Initially, this plea gained widespread support within the Labour movement but was evidently losing its appeal by the 12 May when the TUC called off the sympathetic strike. There were no guarantees about the wages and conditions of employment of the miners, and no undertaking from the Prime Minister that those workers who had come out in support of the miners would not be victimised. At face value, it appears that the most dramatic example of class loyalty in British history ended in ignominy and defeat for the whole trade union movement. Indeed, as one frustrated miner stated, and his views may reflect the opinions of the many, that 'It [the TUC] didn't have much support before the strike but it had less after.'[3]

Writers have been fascinated by the General Strike and have written extensively on its causes, meticulously recorded its events, and speculated about the consequence of its collapse for subsequent British industrial relations. In 1976, on the fiftieth anniversary of the dispute, several important books appeared on the subject, producing almost a surfeit of published research to complement that which had been written, by and large, in the late 1920s and in the early 1970s.[4] Since then there has been no monumental contribution to our understanding of the event, although there have been many local studies, pamphlets and minor publications produced which have not always been easily accessible to the general reader.[5] Recent research has widened our understanding of the dispute and historians are now far more aware of the factors which led to conflict, the local and regional variations in response that occurred, and the consequence of the collapse of the General Strike. Indeed, it is now time for an historiographical update on the current state of our knowledge.

Historians have hotly debated the reasons for the General Strike, measuring the impact of the poor industrial relations in the coal industry against the policies of the TUC and the government. They have also attempted to estimate the effectiveness, or ineffectiveness, of the strike organisation. They disagree about the consequences of the dispute, some suggesting that there was a fundamental change in the direction of trade union policy whilst others maintain that there was a continuity in such policy and the pattern of industrial relations. Indeed, the militancy of the 1920s is often compared with the relative quiescence of the trade union action in the 1930s. But are such observations justified? Did unemployment, economic depression and the General Strike reduce trade unionism to pitiful weakness? Had the trajectory of industrial history been altered by the events of 1926? Can the General Strike be seen, in any case, as the revolutionary strike which the Communists envisaged? And was it a watershed in British industrial relations?

The purpose of this book is to examine the above questions and to focus upon four central debates connected with the causes, events and consequences of the General Strike. The first, which concerns the reasons for conflict, has produced the greatest variety of interpretations. In essence five have emerged, focusing upon the problems of the coal industry, the industrial militancy of the years from 1910 onwards, the influence of the Communist Party of Great Britain, the determination of Baldwin's Conservative government to reduce wage costs and the commitment of the General Council of the TUC to defend the wages of all workers. Some of these arguments seem spurious to say the least. Despite the best efforts of James Klugmann and Robin Page Arnot, the Communist Party of Great Britain's influence appears to have been casual rather than causal, for it carried very little influence, other than in the one or two communities, such as Battersea, which had a Communist MP.[6] The notion that the General Strike was in some way a culmination of the industrial militancy which began in about 1910 is also fallacious. It is a myth which has been destroyed both by the fact that strike activity was

3

declining during the early 1920s and as a result of the evidence that employers and trade unionists were actively involved in reducing the levels of industrial conflict from about 1916 onwards.[7]

More persuasive have been the arguments put forward by Gordon Phillips, who suggests that from 1921 onwards the newly-created General Council of the TUC was determined to instil trade union unity at a time when Baldwin's Conservative government was determined to reduce wage costs and when the coal industry was facing serious industrial conflict.[8] Patrick Renshaw and Margaret Morris, both of whom have written extensively on the causes of the dispute, have not veered markedly from this interpretation. Of course, there was much contemporary exaggeration of the purpose, and thus the causes, of the dispute. The Prime Minister, Stanley Baldwin, saw it in terms of a revolutionary challenge: 'The General Strike is a challenge to Parliament and is the road to anarchy and ruin.'[9] The TUC, which always referred to the strike as 'an industrial dispute in support of the miners' merely retorted that 'The General Council does not challenge the Constitution.'[10] Indeed, they did not wish to do so, although they could not ignore the political and constitutional repercussions which would emerge from a victory over the Government. And one should not ignore the importance of the term the 'General Strike' which had long-established revolutionary connotations in British and European industrial history.

A second debate revolves around the events of the strike and its overall effectiveness before it was called off. Emile Burns maintained that the local organisation of the strike was chaotic.[11] Yet, at the end of the dispute, Fenner Brockway and many activists found it difficult to believe their ears when it was announced that the General Strike had been called off without a settlement to the mining dispute.[12] The perceptions of those directly involved in the dispute obviously differed but recent local research suggests that Emile Burns' analysis was not far from the mark, although the effectiveness of the local councils of action and the Conservative Government and its local administration is still under close scrutiny and the effects of the weakness of organisation may have been offset by class commitment.[13]

Nevertheless, the crunch question, which forms the basis of the third major debate, is not about the effectiveness of the strike but why it was called off? The Communist Party accused the TUC of perpetrating the greatest betrayal in the history of the working class of the world:

> The response of the workers was beyond all praise. The leadership was beneath contempt.
>
> Once called, the strike should have been readily extended. The General Council hesitated, groping for an excuse to end the strike.[14]

A. J. Cook made a similar point, emphasising that the Negotiating Committee of the TUC wished to 'smooth things over' and persuade their colleagues on the General Council to call off the dispute:

> They began to win over one after another of their colleagues on the General Council. Bit by bit the process of 'persuading' the others went on until the situation of complete surrender had been reached, the situation with which we are now faced. It was more than a surrender on their part. It was an ultimatum to us miners, bidding us surrender, too. [15]

The TUC defended itself by suggesting that it had gone as far as it could in supporting the miners and the agreement made by Sir Herbert Samuel, the Samuel Memorandum, would have proved an acceptable basis for a settlement had both the miners and the Conservative government accepted its terms. However, the diaries and letters of Walter Citrine, the acting general secretary of the TUC at that time, suggest that there was an underlying pessimism within TUC ranks which was driving the TUC to compromise and that 'We [the General Council of the TUC] had visions of 1921 in our minds.'[16] Why, then, did the General Council of the TUC call off the dispute? Was it simply because the TUC had made its symbolic gesture, and saw no prospect of victory, or was it simply that it recognised that it could not win?

The fourth debate concerns the consequences of the failure of the General Strike. Did it, for good or ill, prove to be a watershed in British working class history? Marxist writers suggest that the General Strike temporarily de-stabilised British imperialism and added to the experience of class conflict for the lower classes.[17] Other historians, such as Alan Bullock and Patrick Renshaw, have maintained that the defeat of the General Strike led to a quiescence in the trade union movement during the rest of the inter-war years. Yet others, such as Gordon Phillips and Hugh A. Clegg, argue that trade unions did not change their overall industrial strategy as a result of the General Strike and that it may have acted as a check to employers in their attempt to reduce wages.[18]

The main purpose of this book is to examine the above arguments in some detail, drawing, where relevant, upon the mounting local evidence that is becoming available. It will present four main claims. First, that both the TUC and the government were on a collision course, despite their hopes for industrial peace, and that the coal dispute provided the flash-point for conflict. Secondly, it maintains that the strike was more effective than is often supposed, even if communications between the TUC and the local organisations left a lot to be desired. Thirdly, that the TUC called off the dispute because it saw no prospect of victory. Fourthly, it is difficult to view the General Strike as a turning point in British industrial relations; rather it enforced the existing trend towards the creation of better industrial relations. Far from being an unmitigated disaster, the General Strike was, in a sense, a victory for it warned employers of the dangers and economic costs which might arise from industrial conflict. Thus, the reduced level of industrial conflict which followed in 1927 and 1928 can be seen just as much as evidence of a new understanding between trade unions and employers as it can be viewed as evidence of the defeat of trade unionism and its industrial militancy.

In essence, then, there was an inevitability about the strike, the trade union organisation was more effective than suggested and there was a determination by all concerned to create an industrial relations system which would avoid such industrial conflict in the future. In the end Citrine anticipated the outcome of the General Strike in his pre-strike anticipation of the need for firmness and unity when he wrote that 'We all felt that if reduction was forced upon the miners, similar reductions would be made throughout practically all industries. There was a common purpose in the trade unions standing together.'[19] By 1925 and 1926 the TUC was firmly committed to that unity, one which ensured that employers would be reluctant to challenge unions unless it was crucial to do so, despite the unconditional surrender of the TUC on 12 May 1926.

Yet the General Strike did not occur in a vacuum and it is important to realise that it also touches upon the wider pattern of social, economic and political relations in inter-war Britain. It is a lens through which can be viewed many of the events which dominated the inter-war years. It reflects upon the impact of the contractionist policies of successive governments who attempted to balance budgets. It also reflects upon government policy towards the declining industries, and particularly upon the policies of rationalisation and re-organisation which emerged strongly in the case of the coal mining dispute. The General Strike also exerted its impact upon the political means of achieving change. Most obviously it reflected upon conflicting attitudes towards social justice and class differences which were to form the basis of much debate in British society during the inter-war years.

Notes

1 W. Citrine, 'Mining Crisis and National Strike', **4**, 1, of the Diaries and Papers of Walter McLennon Citrine, Baron Citrine of Wembley, deposited in the London School of Economics Library.

2 E. Bevin, *Trade Circular and General Reporter of the AUBTW*, June 1926.

3 Mr. W. Scott, a Scottish miner, interviewed and taped at Halifax, 1 March 1979.

4 M. Morris, *The General Strike*, Journeyman Press, London 1976; M. Morris, *The British General Strike 1926*, Historical Association, London, 1973; G. A. Phillips, *The General Strike: The Politics of Industrial Conflict*, Weidenfeld and Nicolson, London, 1976; P. Renshaw, *The General Strike*, Eyre Methuen, London, 1975; J. Skelley, ed., *The General Strike, 1926*, Lawrence and Wishart, London, 1976. Earlier books include R. Page Arnot, *The General Strike, May 1926: Its Origins and History*, Labour Research Department, London,1926; Emile Burns, *The General Strike, May 1926: Trades Councils in Action*, Labour Research Department, London, 1926; A. J. Cook, *The Nine Days: The story of the Miners' Strike told by the Miners' Secretary*, Miners' Women and Children Fund, Cooperative Printing Society, London, 1926; W. H. Crook, *The General Strike*, University of North Carolina, North Carolina, 1931; C. Farman, *The General Strike, May 1926*, Rupert Hart-Davis, London, 1972; H. Fyfe, *Behind the Scenes of the Great Strike*, Labour Publishing Co., London, 1926; J. Klugmann, *History of the Communist Party, II: The General Strike 1925 – 1926*, Lawrence and Wishart, London, 1969; R. W. Postgate, Ellen Wilkinson and J. F. Horrabin, eds, *A Worker's History of the Great Strike*,

Blackfriar Press, London, 1927; and J. Symons, *The General Strike*, Cresset Press, London, 1957. In addition there are numerous autobiographies by the main participants and prominent politicians.

5   Amongst the most important and useful are D. E. Baines and R. Bean, 'The General Strike on Merseyside', in J. R. Harris, ed., *Liverpool and Merseyside*, F. Cass, London, 1966; R. P. Hastings, 'Aspects of the General Strike in Birmingham 1926', *Midland History*, II, pp. 250–73; R. I. Hills, *The General Strike in York, 1926*, Borthwick Papers, 57, York, 1980; A. Mason, *The General Strike in the North East*, University of Hull, Hull, 1970; J. H. Porter, 'Devon and the General Strike, 1926', *International Review of Social History*, 23, 3, 1978, pp. 333–48; A. R. Williams, 'The General Strike in Gloucestershire', *Transactions of the Bristol and Gloucestershire Archaeological Society*, 91, 1979, pp. 207–13; T. Woodhouse, 'The General Strike in Leeds', *Northern History*, 18, 1982, pp. 252–62; P. Wyncoll, 'The General Strike in Nottingham', *Marxism Today*, **16**, June, 1972.

6   This was Sharpurti Saklatvala, MP. Look at R. Mace, 'The Strike in the Regions: Battersea, London', in Morris, *The General Strike*, pp. 379–93.

7   C. Wrigley, ' Trade Unionists, Employers and the Cause of Industrial Unity and Peace, 1916–1921', in C. Wrigley and J. Shepherd, eds, *On the Move: Essays in Labour and Transport History presented to Philip Bagwell*, Hambledon Press, London, 1991.

8   Phillips, *General Strike*.

9   S. Baldwin, Prime Minister, 6 May 1926, quoted in many newspapers, including *Leeds Mercury*, 7 May 1926.

10   TUC Statement, 7 May 1927, also published in many newspapers.

11   Burns, *General Strike*.

12   Farman, *General Strike*, p. 237.

13   Refer for instance to T. Woodhouse, 'Leeds'.

14   Communist Party of Great Britain (CPGB) statement adopted by the Executive Committee, 29–31 May, 1926, *Workers' Weekly*, 4 June 1926.

15   Cook, *Nine Days*.

16   Citrine, 'Mining Crisis and National Strike', p. 185.

17   J. Foster,' British Imperialism and the Labour Aristocracy', in Skelley, *General Strike*, pp. 3–57.

18   A. Bullock, *The Life and Times of Ernest Bevin; I, Trade Union Leader 1881–1940*, Heinemann, London, 1960; Phillips, *General Strike*, and H. A. Clegg, *A History of British Trade Unionism since 1889, II, 1911–1933*, Clarendon Press, Oxford, 1985, particularly chapters 10 and 14.

19   Citrine, 'Mining Crisis and National Strike', p. 3.

1

Not 'out of a clear sky': the long-term causes of the General Strike

More than sixty years ago, in his classic study of the general strike as a weapon, W. H. Crook wrote that:

> The British general strike of 1926 may have taken the public by surprise and seems to have found even the leaders of labor very unprepared, but it was no surprise to the British Government, nor, to impartial historians, can it be said to have burst upon the world out of a clear sky. Ten years of labor history can claim the making of the great strike, and without the story of that decade a mere description of the actual stoppage would be as futile as it would be unintelligible.[1]

Indeed, although the General Strike had its immediate origins in the miners' lockout of 1926 the long-term events which led to it go back at least to the First World War, during which the coal industry fell under the control of the wartime Coalition Government. Whether its origins go back further is a matter of some conjecture. The fact is that writers and historians have offered a wide range of explanations for the dispute, focusing upon the problems of the mining industry, the TUC and the Conservative Government, although it is doubtful whether any one explanation will suffice.

Interpretations

Some historians have seen the General Strike as the culmination of the period of militant activity which had first begun in 1910.

This owes much to the fact that the syndicalist activities, which began in earnest in 1910, conjured up the vision of a general strike of all industrial unions, once they were formed, as the way in which to overthrow British capitalist society.

The idea of the general strike as a revolutionary weapon had first emerged in Britain in the early nineteenth century, when it was advocated by the Quaker and Radical pamphleteer William Benbow. He set out his ideas in 1832 and argued that only the few enjoyed leisure and pleasure and that the majority toiled. To rectify this situation he advocated a 'Grand National Holiday', or stoppage of labour, which would last until the workers were granted equal rights to the fruits of their labour. Yet his ideas went into abeyance in Britain, after the failures of strikes in the 1830s and the 'grand holiday' of 1842, only to re-emerge in France in the late nineteenth century when George Sorel developed them further in his *Reflections on Violence* and when the Charter of Amiens, of 1906, gave them further credence. The French syndicalist ideas which emerged emphasised the need to work within trade unions, to create industrial unions, to form a parliament of such unions and to call a general strike to overthrow capitalist society.

These ideas were imported back into Britain when Tom Mann developed his Industrial Syndicalist Education League in 1910 and associated them with the amalgamation movement which was occurring at that time. *The Miners' Next Step*, published in March 1912 and written by Noah Ablett and A. J. Cook, the Miners' Federation of Great Britain secretary during the General Strike, was the apogee of these syndicalist ideas in Britain and the movement had more or less expired by the beginning of the First World War. Nevertheless, syndicalism certainly worried contemporary British opinion, especially when the Triple Alliance, a loose association for support in strikes between the unions of the railwaymen, the transport workers and dockers, and the miners, was contemplated in 1914 and formalised in 1915. Yet its influence was marginal to British industrial relations.

There are many problems with the suggestion that syndicalism and the theory of the national holiday played any significant part in the General Strike of 1926. In the first case few historians, other than Bob Holton, would maintain that syndicalism exerted much impact on British trade unionism.[2] The true measure of its influence could be seen, even if in exaggerated form, when Tom Mann failed to secure even a quarter of the vote when he stood for the general secretaryship of the Amalgamated Society of Engineers in 1913.[3] It is true that industrial militancy did occur throughout the First World War and beyond but it peaked in 1921, with nearly eighty-six million working days lost, and the increased number of days lost because of the 1926 General Strike ran counter to the downward trend in industrial conflict.[4] And there is recent evidence, from Chris Wrigley, that trade unionists were moving away from industrial conflict after the First World War. Indeed, Wrigley argues that:

> Among a significant number of trade unionists the experience of wartime cooperation with employers, combined with a distaste for the new militancy, reinforced a pre-war taste for joint committees and for the settling of industrial differences within industries without recourse to Whitehall. This tendency also revealed itself in the participation of many trade unionists, nationally and locally, in forming alliances with employers' organisations in order to propagate the cause of industrial peace and cooperation. During the period of maximum industrial and social unrest bodies such as the National Alliance of Employers and Employed (NAEE) and the Industrial League campaigned vigorously in many of Britain's industrial centres. While the trade unionists of national standing who busied themselves in these organisations were often of second or third-rate importance, leading Labour Party figures – notably J. R. Clynes and Arthur Henderson – did bless the organisations and their effort.[5]

It would appear that by 1926 the trend was firmly moving towards industrial peace. Indeed, Paul Davies suggests, in his recent biography of A. J. Cook, that the syndicalist and revolutionary Cook would have willingly forsaken syndicalist hopes for 'economic security and justice for the men he represented' in 1926.[6]

If syndicalism and industrial militancy offer little in the way of explanation how are we to view the claims of the Communists? Marxist writers have often argued that the CPGB exerted some influence on the event, even if the TUC and trade union leaders let the working class down through their collaboration with the existing capitalist system. This type of view has been clearly enunciated by James Klugmann, the historian of the CPGB, who has indicated the way in which the Communist Party struggled to

Table 1   *Disputes and the number of days lost 1909–1926*

Year	Disputes	Days Lost (000s)
1909	422	2,690,000
1910	521	9,870,000
1911	872	10,160,000
1912	834	40,890,000
1913	1,459	9,800,000
1914	972	9,880,000
1915	672	2,950,000
1916	532	2,450,000
1917	730	5,650,000
1918	1,165	5,880,000
1919	1,352	34,970,000
1920	1,607	26,570,000
1921	763	85,870,000
1922	576	19,850,000
1923	628	10,670,000
1924	710	8,420,000
1925	603	7,950,000
1926	323	162,230,000

politicise the trade union movement.[7] How pervasive this influence was is hard to measure for whilst there were Communists, such as Robin Page Arnot, active in the strike, their influence appears to have been very localised and limited. They supported a policy of 'All Power to the General Council' in the months leading up to the dispute but carried almost no influence on the General Council. Their claim to influencing events through A. J. Cook, the secretary of the Miners' Federation of Great Britain, also has a hollow ring about it since Cook had left the CPGB in September 1921, shortly after its formation, due to its involvement in the 1921 coal strike. At that time Cook complained of the interference of the Communist Party in the lock-out and described the Communists as 'a hindrance to the whole of the British Trade Union Movement'.[8] And it may well be, as Tony Lane suggests, that Communist influence was limited by the possibility that 'trade unionism on its own carried within itself a politics of accommodation to a capitalist society'.[9] In truth, Communism does not appear to have carried much influence before, during or after the General Strike.

If industrial militancy and the work of the CPGB carry little weight what long-term factors did cause the General Strike? The consensus of opinion suggests that three other factors – the government, the trade unions/TUC and the conditions in the coal industry – were far more important. Offering a synthesis of these ideas, the general thrust of argument is that the First World War strengthened a trade union movement which was prepared to resist the wage encroachments of employers, who were faced with both the increasingly competitive demands of the world markets and the rationalising policies of successive governments, during the immediate post-war years. In this climate poor industrial relations in the mining industry worsened by the debate over ownership of the industry as a whole, unleashed many of the tensions which underlay industrial relations in the early 1920s. In other words, the new pattern of industrial relations was unstable. In general outline this type of argument is supported by Margaret Morris, Patrick Renshaw, Gordon Phillips and many others,[10] although they all offer their own particular variant. Of these, perhaps the most persuasive is the explanation offered by Phillips that the TUC's industrial policy was one of commitment to the need for trade unity. However, he also argues that the TUC was forced into precipitate action in 1926 by the need to expiate the guilt of 1921, when on 'Black Friday', 15 April 1921, the Triple Alliance failed to support the miners in their strike against wage reductions.[11]

Government, the employers, the coal industry and the TUC 1918–1925

The First World War marked a sharp break in the history of trade unionism, raising trade unions to a new level of importance. Most obviously, it saw the rapid rise of trade union membership from four millions in 1914 to six millions in 1918. By 1920 the figure was more than eight millions. The high demand for labour, high wartime wages and the government's need to work with the trade unions were vital wartime factors which greatly strengthened the trade union movement. Employers were keenly aware of these changes. For instance, a meeting of the North London Manufacturers' Association on 16 July 1918 was told that 'the industrial system of this country, as we knew it in July 1914, has been suspended' and that it was 'unlikely to be re-established without modification of a far-reaching nature'. Specifically, 'no part of the pre-war industrial system is more likely to be radically changed in design and practice after the war than the relationship between employers and employed.'[12] There was widespread acknowledgement that some industrial power had been conceded to the trade unions in order to win the war. It was also obvious that the impetus which the trade unions gained would lead to conflict once attempts were made, by government and employers alike, to abandon wartime regulations and to return to the competitive situation of the pre-war world, despite the contrary moves towards industrial peace that were being nurtured.

Industrial conflict became increasingly likely after 1920 when unemployment rose quickly, due to the failure of British trade to recover to its pre-war level. Faced with intense foreign competition, employers resorted to attempts to reduce monetary wages, eventually encouraged by the decisions of Baldwin's Conservative government, in 1925, to return to the gold standard and to reflate the pound. Indeed it was these actions which increased the price of British exports, encouraged employers to attempt to reduce the wages of workers, and provoked the the coal lock-out of 1926 and the resultant General Strike. A galvanised trade union movement facing the problems of high unemployment and constant wage reductions was inevitably going to be in conflict with both employers and government during the inter-war years, if only because its enlarged membership was expecting it to defend their position. This is ironic, since successive political leaders in government had come to a view that the mass of workers had gone 'red' and that it was only the trade union leaders who were holding back the threat of revolution: Winston Churchill lamented, in February 1919, that 'The curse of trade unionism was that there was not enough of it, and it was not highly enough developed to make its branch secretaries fall into line with head office.'[13] The government's fear was not that there would be a general strike, not that there would be revolution, but, as H. A. Clegg has suggested, that a coalition of local leaders would take control of national decision-making and prevent the national union leaders from reaching compromises acceptable to both the employers and government, because they had greater expectation of what could be achieved by industrial action. In the end government action prevented trade unions adopting the moderating role which some in government hoped that they would assume.

The immediate post-war governments set a course of action in motion which threatened to undermine the power of the trade unions. John Foster argues the orthodox Marxist line that the post-war governments faced a crisis in capitalism and imperialism, following the First World War, which could only be retrieved by an attack upon wages: 'The attack on the miners was part of a general drive to reduce wages, to force all workers to bear the costs of British banking hegemony.'[14] Although Foster's subsequent argument is conditioned by a rigid Marxist framework, his general contention that successive governments were committed to reducing wages would appear to be correct. The fact is that they were committed to such a course of action by their adherence to the implementation of the report of the Cunliffe Committee on Currency and Foreign Exchange (1918).[15] This report advocated that Britain should strengthen the pound to its pre-war parity against the dollar and return Britain to the gold standard within seven years – which it did in 1925. It advocated a battery of actions, including the balancing of the budget, the legal limitation of note issue and the repayment of the National Debt. The net result of all this was that there was deflation, unemployment increased, costs were reduced and wages fell. It was perhaps not surprising that, in 1925, Stanley Baldwin, the then Conservative Prime Minister, should suggest that wages would have to fall. As one Yorkshire newspaper suggested after the textile workers had fought off wage reductions in 1925:

> Wages, said Mr Baldwin, have to be brought down. This is not simply an uncautious and unconsidered statement by Mr Baldwin, a slip of the tongue: it is the settled and deliberate policy of the governing class, who have entered upon a course of action which has for its object the deliberate intensification of unemployment as a method of forcing down wages.[16]

Government economic policy was quite clearly geared towards confrontation with the trade unions, even if there was the hope that industrial peace would be maintained through trade union leaders. This situation was potentially worsened by the fact that the government retained control of the mining and railway industries until 1921, which meant that it was directly involved in both determining the futures of these industries and in industrial negotiations. No longer could governments stand back from industrial relations since their decisions were most likely to affect their development – even though, as Rodney Lowe has suggested, governments were intent upon gradually withdrawing from industrial relations.[17] This was particularly evident in the case of the coal industry which was given back to the coal owners in April 1921. The decision to do so has become infamous in Labour history for it arose from the attempt of the Prime Minister, David Lloyd George, to avoid industrial conflict in mining, setting up a Royal Commission, the Sankey Commission, to determine whether to nationalise the industry or to return it to the coal owners, and offering to accept the majority verdict. Most miners looked aghast at the Government's subsequent decision to reject the Sankey Commission's decision to nationalise and to return the industry to the coal owners. In early 1919, Vernon Hartshorn, the South Wales miners' leader, angrily enquired in the House of Commons:

> Why was the commission set up? Was it a huge game of bluff? Was it ever intended that if the reports favoured nationalisation we were to get it? . . . That is the kind of question the miners of the country will ask, and they will say they have been deceived, betrayed, duped.[18]

Governments also interfered in other respects as well. The First World War had led to the introduction of the Defence of the Realm Act (DORA) and had provided the government with a battery of controls to regulate industrial relations. Indeed, in February 1919 a Cabinet committee on industrial unrest was set up. It was later extended and became known as the Strike Committee during the transport strike in September 1919. In October 1919 it became the Supply and Transport Committee under Sir Eric Geddes, the Chief Civil Commissioner. Responsible to the Cabinet, it created special divisional offices in the regions and worked with public and voluntary bodies. In addition, it operated within the Emergency Powers Act which had been introduced due to a miners' strike in October 1920. It gave power to the executive, on the declaration of a state of emergency, to introduce temporary but legally binding regulations by order-in-council to preserve the peace and maintain essential supplies. However, once the Triple Alliance (an industrial alliance organised between the Miners' Federation of Great Britain, the National Union of Railwaymen and the National Transport Workers' Federation) collapsed on 'Black Friday', 15 April 1921 and the Lloyd George Government had returned coal and transport back to the employers, the Supply and Transport Committee also practically collapsed. However it was revived in May 1923 by Stanley Baldwin, who appointed J. C. C. Davidson to organise its responsibilities. He began the process of rebuilding the government's anti-strike organisation, the very organisation which the TUC faced during the General Strike of 1926.

Yet if governments prepared to meet the threat of strike activity which resulted from their policies, the employers were almost equally determined to reduce the costs of production, and thus wages, in the face of intense foreign competition. Indeed, employers constantly gnawed away at the high level of wages which had been built up during the First World War. They frequently attempted to reduce the basic wage of workers and to eliminate the cost of living addition which had been paid since the beginning of the war. Indeed, one estimate suggests that the wages of Britain's workers were reduced by about £12 million per week between 1921 and 1925.[19] But this had not improved Britain's competitive position, and all that such wage cuts had done was to reduce the home demand for products, thus further increasing unemployment. Ben Turner, of the General Union of Textile Workers and soon to be president of the TUC, wrote in 1925 that:

> It's as much home trade we are suffering from as a lack of foreign trade. In fact the reduction in home trade is far bigger than the reduction in exports, and this is accounted for by the ten million reduction a week that has occurred during 1920–1–2. That ten million paid out now would give a right big fillip to trade.[20]

Trade unionists had increasingly come to accept that under-consumption was the cause of stagnant trade, for, as stated by the *Manifesto* of the woollen textile workers, issued on the eve of the 1925 textile lock-out: 'There is no greater fallacy today than to think we could get back to prosperity by reducing wages.'[21]

Not all employers were as aggressive towards their workers as

17

those in mining and textiles. Chris Wrigley has emphasised that there were determined attempts to create industrial unity and peace, especially between 1916 and 1921. Similar sentiments were abroad in the steel industry of which Frank Wilkinson has suggested, in his detailed study of its collective bargaining, that 'Despite this lapse during the General Strike the industry maintained its reputation for peacefully resolving its own wage disputes during the 1920s.'[22]

Nevertheless, in many basic industries which were facing industrial decline the employers adopted a strategy of forcing wages down. In the years 1920 and 1921, which, respectively, saw British industry lose 26,568,000 and 85,872,000 days in strikes, wages were forced down and trade union membership fell by about 1.8 million – the most rapid decline that occurred in any period during the inter-war years. That decline in wages and trade union membership was most pronounced in the coal industry, which was wracked by industrial conflict.

The coal industry was vital in the brew of industrial relations which led to the General Strike, even before the immediate crisis of 1925 and 1926. The industry had become subject to government control during the First World War. After the war the leading question in the mining industry was would the state return the coal mines to the coal owners? The MFGB, which had passed resolutions in favour of both workers' control and nationalisation, supported continued state control and, in order to avoid industrial conflict, the Lloyd George Coalition Government set up a royal commission, chaired by Lord Sankey, to investigate the industry. Although the Sankey Commission produced four different reports, the majority one – on the casting vote of the chairman – recommended that the coal industry should continue under national control. Lloyd George, reneging upon a former promise to implement the Majority Report, decided to return the mines to the coal owners. The consequence was immediate; the Yorkshire miners struck, unsuccessfully, in July 1919 and some 200,000 miners in South Wales and Monmouth threatened sympathetic strike action, although it never occurred. In the final analysis, this sympathetic support did not emerge. Yet the frustration which this 'betrayal' caused among the coal miners was to dominate the industry for many years to come. As one historian has noted: 'The bitterness and the troubles of the coal mines for the next seven, or for that matter twenty-seven years, derived in great part from the feeling of both miners and owners that they had been betrayed.'[23]

Although there were several disputes in the coal industry during the next twenty months, it was not until the coal mines were formally handed back to the coal owners, on 31 March 1921, that serious conflict ensued. On the following day, the coal owners locked out those miners who would not work at lower rates of pay – of up to forty-nine per cent off in the badly affected export areas of South Wales – and attempted to suspend national agreements. The government also issued regulations under the 1920 Emergency Powers Act and recalled troops from Ireland and abroad to quell the miners and their supporters. The government feared that the Triple Alliance, might be used to widen the dispute. It need not have feared.

The expected support of the NUR and the NTW evaporated away on 15 April 1921, on a day now known as 'Black Friday'. Although Ernest Bevin's transport workers had not come out on strike the opprobrium of the trade union movement was directed at Jimmy Thomas, the leader of the railwaymen, whose opposition to sympathetic strike action was considered to be the cause of the collapse of the Triple Alliance. He had not helped his cause when he 'trotted blithely down the steps to greet eager reporters with the news "It's all off boys" and added, to cries of "Jimmy's selling you" the riposte "I've tried boys, I've done my very best. But I couldn't find a bloody buyer." '[24]

The immediate outcome of the collapse of the Triple Alliance was that the miners were left to fight alone. Eventually, they were forced to accept some significant wage reductions and sliding scale arrangements, whereby wages were to form about 85 per cent of the difference between the cost of production (including basic or standard wages) and gross receipts. Nevertheless, wage levels remained reasonable as a result of the French invasion of the Ruhr and the American coal strike of 1924. Indeed, the 1924 wage agreement saw the wage percentage on net proceeds rise to eighty-seven per cent. It was not until 1925 that the downward pressure on wages was again to produce the threat of a major industrial conflict in the coalfields.

It was 'Black Friday' that forced the TUC to change its organisation to deal effectively with the attack of the employers and the general strategy adopted by government. Partly in consequence, the TUC was forced to form the General Council, an alternative to its parliamentary committee, as its executive body. Moves towards forming such a body had been made in the immediate post-war years and were finally endorsed by the Congress of 1921. Although initially having few statutory powers, it was given the task of dealing with inter-union disputes, assisting the improvement of organisation, watching legislation in the interest of labour, and also the task of co-ordinating industrial action by the unions and 'to assist any union which is attacked on any vital question of Trade Union principle'.[25] The real purpose of the General Council was, therefore, to establish trade unity and to intervene in major industrial disputes. In 1922 it set up a Joint Defence Committee, later known as the Committee for Coordination of Trade Union Effort, to accomplish this aim. Yet it was not until the Hull Congress of 1924 that it was effectively strengthened, when Fred Bramley was appointed full-time secretary, with Walter Citrine as assistant-secretary, and when it was given extra statutory powers. The General Council established contact with the trades councils through a Joint Consultative Committee, with the aim of converting them to local publicity agencies and, for the first time, mediated in industrial disputes which involved shipbuilding workers, dockers, builders and railwaymen.[26]

This strengthening of the General Council meant that it had at last won the confidence of the trades union movement. Prior to 1924 it had gained limited support from the unions, particularly the MFGB and the NUR who suspected that it might act to discourage and control, rather than to encourage, strike action. But from 1924 onwards its powers were extended in a debate which saw the miners and other unions switch their support to it. The reason for this change of attitude has been the subject of debate, on the one hand, between B. C. Roberts and J. Lovell, who feel that the new Standing Orders, which strengthened the Council, were a product of a switch in the attitude of the Left, and Phillips who feels that it was simply that unions changed their minds and that with the changed nature of the General Council's demands unions simply accepted the need to strengthen the General Council's Standing Orders.[27]

In 1925 some of the leading trade unions also began to consider the possibility of an Industrial Alliance. The MFGB, faced with the impending threat of major industrial conflict, joined with Transport and General Workers' Union to express support for the ultimately futile attempt to establish such an alliance. The real problem was that all the participating unions were guarding their own sectional interests. The MFGB were concerned about immediate threats, the Federation of Engineering and Shipbuilding Trades ultimately withdrew because the Industrial Alliance threatened to disrupt the conduct of peaceful negotiations with their employers and only Ernest Bevin, and the TGWU, appear to have contemplated the possibility of a permanent Alliance. Indeed, as a TGWU conference in July 1925 he stated that:

> I am sorry, really, that this Alliance comes just at the time of the miners' difficulty. I would rather it be discussed apart from that. We do not think we ought, simply because we have an instrument like this, to be striking every minute. With the Alliance we would have bargaining power that we do not at present possess. If there was an Alliance of this character in being it would not be permitted to side-step. It could act with tremendous bargaining power and probably lift the whole thing out of the rut it might be in. [28]

The fact that the General Council gave support to the miners in the coal dispute of 1925 gave further credence to the idea of an Industrial Alliance, whilst masking the fact that the Alliance was never actually forged and that the General Council was making its own efforts in that direction. The scent of battle was sufficient to strengthen the hand of the, normally reluctant, General Council which was further galvanised when the Communist Party put forward its slogan 'All Power to the General Council'.

Various circumstances contrived to ensure that the General Council had to take more determined action to defend its members in 1925. In the first place, unemployment was well in excess of a million and had helped to reduce wages. Secondly, the situation seemed to be worsening as the coal industry faced the difficulties of declining demand. Thirdly, Baldwin's Conservative government had decided to return to the gold standard and to reflate the pound in April 1925, the implication being that costs, and hence wages, would have to fall by about ten per cent if British industry was to remain competitive as it had been at the old rates of exchange. There was, in addition, the experience of the woollen and worsted workers in the textile belt of the West Riding of Yorkshire, whose determined stand against wage cuts brought renewed hope to the trade union movement.

The wool and worsted textile dispute, 1925

The wool and worsted textile workers were amongst the least well-organised of all industrial workers, but had enjoyed a 'cosy relationship' with their employers through the existence of a Whitley Council which, had been formed during the First World War to settle disputes by negotiation. Suddenly, in the summer of 1925, they faced a serious challenge from the employers who wished to reduce wages. This was hardly the most propitious moment for the textile unions to make their stand. Yet, in April 1925 the Executive Committee of the National Union of Textile Workers declared its intention of demanding the restoration of the five per cent on base wages lost in 1921 and that the cost of living addition should be altered every three months – an action which would greatly benefit the textile workers. These demands were endorsed by the National Association of Unions in the Textile Trade and the matter was put to the employers who responded by suggesting that British industry was less competitive than it had been before the return of the gold standard and the reflation of the pound, and suggested that wages should be reduced by ten, later reducing to eight and five, per cent.[29]

The seeds of conflict were sown and, despite offers of mediation from several quarters, the employers issued notices of wage reductions on 24 July 1925, when a lock-out began.[30] It lasted just over three weeks and the immediate conflict was only resolved by the intervention of the Minister of Labour, Sir Arthur Steel-Maitland, who requested that the employers allow the existing wage rates to continue until a Court of Investigation, which had been set up, reported upon the wool and worsted textile trades. When that body, which was composed of an independent chairman and two representatives from each side, eventually reported, it opted for a preservation of the *status quo*.[31]

The importance of this dispute should not be lost. In the first place, there were probably between 135,000 and 170,000 workers involved, although some estimates go up to 240,000, and every union and all sections of the textile workforce were unified in the action they took. Ben Turner, the main trade union leader and a subsequent president of the TUC, was pleased to reflect that:

> I am glad to have lived to see the day when overlookers, foremen and managers, craftsmen, engine tenters, etc. joined together to defend labour's interests – when the doffer lass, the designer, the long brat men, and the woolcombers were standing together.[32]

Such unity was remarkable in an industry which was notorious for its local variation, the disunity of its workforce and the general weakness of its trade union organisation.

Secondly, the outcome of the dispute was seen as a victory for the workers in their attempt to prevent wages being reduced further. Even before the Court of Investigation confirmed the workers' stand, the trade unions had smelled the scent of victory. On the eve of the agreement to call off the dispute, the *Yorkshire Factory Times* reflected that the wage retreat had at last 'been stopped'.[33]

Combined with a temporary solution to the coal crisis in 1925, which will be discussed later, the anticipated textile victory buoyed up the whole of the trade union movement. Herbert Tracey reflected that the 'defeatist' mood of the trade unions over the last few years had been transformed. Now it was felt that the General Council of the TUC had struck a blow to maintain minimum wages for all workers by its support of the woollen and worsted textile workers. But the message went further for it was felt that the lesson to be learned was that living standards could be protected if unity prevailed: 'With the help of the Trade Union Movement, mobilised by the T.U.C. General Council, they were enabled to secure victory which they could not have won if they were left to fight alone.'[34]

The moral seemed obvious: the reversal of the onslaught on wages and the defence of a minimum wage, if not the establishment of a living wage, could be secured by an alliance among unions. It was felt that if such unity could be achieved in the poorly organised wool textile trade then it was even more likely that it might be achieved in the better-organised industries. Indeed, the temporary settlement of the coal dispute of 1925, which occurred at more or less the same time, appeared to confirm this impression. There was, indeed, growing support for collective action within unions in specific industries and between the unions of all industries – something which the TUC encouraged through its new journal *Trade Union Unity*.

Conclusion

Although there was nothing particularly inevitable about the General Strike occurring in 1926 – and many have enquired into why it did not occur in 1921 – it is clear that the Government and the TUC were sliding towards conflict. Whilst successive governments saw the need to reduce wages as part of the process of making Britain more competitive it is equally obvious that the TUC was, with grudging support, moving towards a situation where it felt impelled to take a stand. Neither the Baldwin Government nor the TUC wished for conflict – the former attempting to intervene in major disputes to defuse potential conflict, whilst the latter was essentially a conservative force harbouring within it the sectional interests of many different unions. Rather it was the vested interests of both the Government and the TUC which drove them on to conflict, and apart from the appropriate preparations, there is little evidence that the eventual conflict was a product of some great plot by the government, the TUC or the Communist Party. Given the competing interests, conflict was likely, if not inevitable, when the coal dispute of 1925 threatened major confrontation.

Notes

1 Crook, *General Strike*, p. 233.

2 B. Holton, *British Syndicalism 1900–1914: Myth and Realities*, Pluto Press, London, 1976.

3 C. Tsuzuki, *Tom Mann 1856–1941: The Challenges of Labouur*, OUP, Oxford, 1991, p. 167.

4 Phillips, *General Strike*, p. 287.

5 Wrigley, 'Trade Unionists', p. 155.

6 P. Davies, *A. J. Cook*, Manchester University Press, Manchester, 1987, p. 98.

7 Klugmann, *Communist Party*.

8 Davies, *Cook*, p. 58.

9 T. Lane, *The Union Makes Us Strong*, Arrow Books, 1974, pp. 15–27.

10 Morris, *General Strike*; Renshaw, *General Strike*; Phillips, *General*

Strike.

11   Phillips, *General Strike*, p. 13.

12   H. B. Graham, *Relations between Employers and Employed* (1918) **1**, 3, *passim*, quoted in J. E. Cronin, 'Coping with Labour 1918–1926' in J. E. Cronin and J. Schneer, eds, *Social Conflict and the Political Order of Modern Britain*, Croom Helm, Beckenham, 1982, p. 115.

13   Quoted in K. Middlemass, *Politics in Industrial Society: The Experience of the British System since 1914*, Andre Deutsch, 1979, pp. 143–4.

14   J. Foster, 'British Imperialism', p. 50.

15   Cd. 9821, HMSO, London, 1918.

16   *Yorkshire Factory Times*, 13 August 1925.

17   R. Lowe, 'The erosion of state intervention in Britain, 1917–24', *Economic History Review*, 31, 1978, pp. 270–86; R. Lowe, 'Government and Industrial Relations, 1919–1939', in C. J. Wrigley, ed., *A History of British Industrial Relations, II, 1914–1939*, Harvester, Brighton, 1987. Also look at J. A. Jowitt and K. Laybourn, 'The Wool Textile Dispute of 1925', *The Journal of (Regional and) Local Studies*, **2**, 1, spring.

18   *Hansard*, 18 August 1919.

19   *Yorkshire Factory Times*, 23 July 1925.

20   *Ibid.*, 28 May 1925.

21   *Manifesto*, Amalgamated Union of Dyers at West Yorkshire Archives, Bradford, Department and the National Union of Textile Workers' collection, West Yorkshire Archives Department, Huddersfield Central Library. Also, *Yorkshire Factory Times*, 23 July 1925.

22   F. Wilkinson, 'Collective Bargaining in the Steel Industry in the 1920s', in A. Briggs and J. Saville, eds, *Essays in Labour History 1918–1939*, Croom Helm, Beckenham, 1977.

23   C. L. Mowat, *Britain between the Wars*, Methuen, London, 1968 edn, p. 34.

24   Renshaw, *General Strike*, p. 87.

25   TUC Standing Orders, 1921.

26   TUC, *Report*, 1924.

27   Phillips, *General Strike*, pp. 17–20.

28   TGWU, Biennial Delegate Conference, 23 July 1925, *Report*, p. 5. Look at the Document section for material on the Industrial Alliance.

29   National Union of Textile Workers' Executive Committee Meeting, Memorandum, E/C/14/249, 4 April 1925, box 2; Amalgamated Union of Dyers, 126 D77/192, National Wool (and Allied) Textile Industrial Council, Minutes, Memorandum IC 196, 18 May 1925 and Memorandum IC 196, 197 and 201; C. Wrigley, *Cosy Co-operation under Strain: Industrial Relations in the Yorkshire Woollen Industry 1919–1930* , Borthwick Papers, University of York, York, 1987.

30   Jowitt, Laybourn, 'Wool Textile Dispute', p. 15.

31   *Yorkshire Factory Times*, 19 November 1925 and the National

Association of Unions in the Textile Trades, *Report of the Court of Investigations concerning the wages position in the Wool Textile Trade (Northern Counties)*, NAUTT, Bradford, 1925, box 32.

32   National Union of Textile Workers, *Quarterly Record*, 11 (October 1925) and also quoted in Wrigley, *Cosy Co-operation*, p. 23.

33   *Yorkshire Factory Times*, 13 August 1925.

34   *Ibid.*, 27 August 1925.

2

The 1925 Coal Crisis and the nine-month respite

Whatever the long-term ingredients of the General Strike, its immediate cause was the threatened conflict within the coal mining industry in July 1925, which elicited from the General Council of the TUC a commitment to defend the wages and working conditions of the miners. Combined with the decision of the Conservative government to provide a temporary nine-month subsidy, to avert the strike, on 'Red Friday', 31 July 1925, the possibility of major industrial conflict in May 1926 looked highly likely. Although these two vital elements ultimately dictated that there would be conflict on a major national scale it is equally clear that the events which led to the General Strike are immensely complex, confused and controversial – most certainly open to wide interpretation. They have raised a number of vital questions. Why, for instance, did the TUC intervene to support the miners when their projected extension of industrial powers was by no means complete? Why did the TUC not prepare for their national strike in support of the miners when it was clear that the Government had used the nine-month armistice to make all the necessary arrangements for conflict? Indeed, was there ever a realistic possibility that the Samuel Commission, set up by the Government to examine the coal industry, would help avert conflict? One possible, and well-evidenced, answer to these questions is that the TUC was haunted by the vision of 'Black Friday', buoyed up by recent industrial successes but complacent when it came to the need for preparation. In essence, there was a recognition of the need for unity but a lack of machinery and commitment to fulfil that need. The point was well made by Walter Citrine, who was acting general secretary of the TUC in 1926, when he wrote that:

> My diary shows that I was much preoccupied after the temporary settlement in 1925 in view of the lack of awareness of the need for preparation in case industrial action became necessary in 1926 . . . We all felt that if reduction was forced upon the miners, similar reductions would be made throughout practically all industries. There was a common purpose in the trade unions standing together.[1]

As Citrine later acknowledged, the pity was that little in the way of preparation was achieved. The General Council, partly through its own pessimism about the coming strike, deluded itself into thinking that it could act as an intermediary between the warring factions. Unfortunately it couldn't, and it found itself supporting the miners against both the coal owners and the Government.

Red Friday, 31 July 1925

The events which led to 'Red Friday' began on 30 June 1925 when the coal owners decided that they would abolish the national minimum wage agreement made in 1924 (whereby eighty-seven per cent of their net receipts, the difference between costs and gross receipts, went to wages) and cut wages by about ten per cent. They decided to maintain standard profits no matter how low wages fell and argued that conditions could be better if the miners were willing to accept the pre-Sankey conditions and work an eight-hour day. The reason for their action was that British coal exports were falling whilst German exports were increasing following the withdrawal of the French from the Ruhr, and that most of the British pits were facing considerable financial losses. Consequently, within a few months of the 1924 wage agreement in the industry all the coal districts, except South Yorkshire, were paying the bare minimum wage rate; South Yorkshire did so from July 1925. The new arrangements were to take place from 1 August 1925.

The coal owners effectively declared war on the coal miners

when they issued their new arrangements on 1 July 1925. The miners rejected the employers' terms at a Special Conference on 3 July 1925 and refused to meet the owners until the new demands were withdrawn. Instead they met the General Council of the TUC on 10 July. During this meeting 'Cook was very animated and vigorous and hammered his point home . . .'[2], after which the Council resolved to 'give their complete support (to the miners), and to cooperate wholeheartedly with them in their resistance to the mine-owners' proposals'.[3] A Special Industrial Committee (SIC) was appointed, with A. J. Swales as chairman, and John Bromley, George Hicks, Arthur Hayday, J. Marchbank, E. L. Poulton, Ben Tillett, A. G. Walkden and Walter Citrine as members. But the arrangement was loose and little action was taken for two weeks. In the meantime the Government attempted to bring the two sides together and, on 11 July, appointed an independent Court of Inquiry under H. P. Macmillan. The miners refused to work with it and, on 20 July, it began its hearings without them. On the 28 July the Macmillan Inquiry published a report which suggested that the industry as a whole needed to be made more efficient and that 'wages at some agreed minimum rate must in practice be a charge before profits are taken'.[4] Obviously, the *Macmillan Inquiry Report* was not going to provide a solution to the crisis, for the coal owners rejected the findings and the miners simply ignored it.

Indeed, it was already evident that, even before the *Macmillan Inquiry Report* was published, the General Council was willing to support the miners in resisting wage reductions. The miners' executive met the SIC on 23 July, when a variety of ideas for help began to emerge. On the following day a Coal Embargo Committee was appointed by the General Council. Thus the General Council had given its, somewhat tentative, support to the miners. But why had it done so? Gordon Phillips suggests that this was because it felt that a stand had to be made against the threat of wage reductions and that a coal embargo might bring a settlement in favour of the miners.[5] This view is strongly endorsed by the evidence presented in the previous chapter and by Citrine who, with other members of the SIC had met the Prime Minister, Stanley Baldwin, on 27 July.

I told Baldwin, very frankly, that we could not allow the miners to be beaten on this issue, and I appealed to him to make a public statement asking the mine owners to withdraw their notices. He said he would do everything he could to get a peaceful settlement. He was taking the matter in hand himself and would see the mine owners tomorrow.[6]

Swales, a left-wing member of the Committee, stated that 'We are out to back the miners and we mean to support them.'[7] But Citrine was also aware of the risk the General Council was taking, given its lack of central authority, the absence of a scientific strike policy, and the 'cumbrous slow-moving Trade Union machine' which would make the calling of a general strike 'a farce'.[8] Nevertheless, the prospect of a TUC embargo on the movement of coal was threatened despite the lack of preparation for its enforcement.

The lack of preparedness of the General Council was only exceeded by that of the Government. It had the machinery to act, in the form of the Emergency Powers Act of 1920, but was undecided on what action to take. Indeed, Philip Cunliffe Lister, the President of the Board of Trade, had warned the Cabinet on 28 May 1925 that there might be a coal strike at the end of July, but his warning had gone almost unheeded.[9] Winston Churchill, Sir William Joynson-Hicks, and other hard-liners, argued that the Government was ready to meet the emergency but that sufficient volunteers could not be found to provide food, transport, fuel, power and communications without the declaration of a State of Emergency. Yet Baldwin did not call a Cabinet meeting to discuss the crisis and Joynson-Hicks's report on the preparations until 23 July.[10] The *Macmillan Inquiry Report* appeared to offer no solution to the problem and Baldwin's meetings with the TUC, the miners and the owners offered no prospect of an amicable settlement.

The last-minute meetings between Baldwin and the coal owners, coal miners and the TUC came to a head at the end of July. On 29 July, Baldwin informed the miners that the coal owners were prepared to offer a low minimum wage. This offer of a reduced wage cut was summarily rejected by the miners' leaders, after brief consultations with the SIC. Other possibilities also emerged. At 9 pm the SIC met the Prime Minister for the second time and asked the Government to provide a subsidy to avert the crisis. Baldwin rejected this idea on the following morning, stating that 'the Government are not prepared to give a subsidy to the industry'.[11] However, that evening there had been a complete reversal of attitudes and a meeting of the Cabinet decided, on a vote, 'that as between the national strike and the payment of assistance to the mining industry, the latter course was less disadvantageous'.[12] The Government decision to provide a subsidy and to set up a royal commission on coal was announced next day, Friday, 31 July 1925, which henceforth became known as 'Red Friday'.

Why had the Prime Minister and the Cabinet changed their position? J. Symons suggests that Baldwin's explanation was correct: 'We were not ready.' Indeed, he argues that the Government machinery for dealing with disputes had been run down once the Labour government assumed power in 1924.[13] Phillips endorses this view, citing the evidence of the Cabinet's concern that volunteers could not be organised in time to deal effectively with the emergency.[14] But Renshaw is not so convinced and suggests that Baldwin's change of mind was due to the fact that he, and the majority of his Cabinet, felt that public sympathy was with the miners and that if conditions improved the crisis might be averted.[15] As Churchill stated, on 10 December 1925, 'We decided to postpone the crisis in the hope of averting it, or, if not averting it, of coping with it when the time came'.[16] There is, indeed, strong evidence for both views. Yet, one must reflect that the Government machinery was there, and ministers could have taken effective action if they had so wished. In this light, Renshaw's explanation appears the more plausible.

The nine-month interregnum

'Red Friday' occupies a special place in British Labour history, not least because it offered the workers a vision of hope in the otherwise bleak landscape of industrial relations. Cook suggested that capitalism could be replaced by socialism and George Hicks believed that Red Friday 'will open the way to a victorious working-class offensive'.[17] But few trade union leaders seem to have been misled about its real meaning. Herbert Smith informed the miners that 'We have no need to glorify about a victory . . . It is only an armistice.'[18] He later wrote that 'The recent crisis was an affair of outposts. It was a mere skirmish. The main battle had to be fought and won.'[19] He shared this view with many others

31

on both the Left and the Right. David Lloyd George anticipated no amicable outcome from a subsidy and a royal commission,[20] Churchill was prepared to meet the situation as it arose, Ramsay MacDonald felt that 'Red Friday' would encourage the revolutionaries to greater efforts,[21] J. H. Thomas wished to avoid future conflict, and Walter Citrine feared that an ill-prepared TUC would be faced with a major crisis.[22] Herbert Tracey reminded:

> enthusiastic Trade Unionists . . . that the movement today, powerful as it is, is not strong enough for the grand assault upon the capitalist citadel which they dream of seeing the Labour Movement make in their lifetime. . . . The Trade Unions will be sufficiently seriously occupied in defending the interests of their members against further encroachments from the employers.[23]

How then did the various parties prepare for the threatened conflict?

It is generally accepted that the Government organised itself far more effectively than did the TUC, and that the trade union preparations at local level reflected the obvious ineptitude of the national movement. But was this so? How effective were Government preparations? How seriously did the TUC take the potential conflict?

There seems little doubt that the Government prepared well for conflict in 1926. Indeed Joynson-Hicks, the Home Secretary, warned that:

> This thing is not finished. The danger is not over. Sooner or later this question has to be fought out by the people of the land. Is England and Parliament to be ruled by a Cabinet or by trade union leaders?[24]

Government ministers were clearly taking matters seriously and were preparing for conflict. And, twenty-five years ago, Tony Mason established the enormous range and magnitude of Government preparations.[25] The Government quickly strengthened its counter-strike organisation administered by the Supply and Transport Committee. The Home Secretary submitted a report on 7 August 1925 which led to expansion of the specialised staff at divisional headquarters of the supply and transport system, and the recruitment of employer representatives in ports and railway centres was absorbed into the official apparatus of state. Resources were to be stockpiled, the national committee of transport established contacts with local authorities and a local voluntary network was set up, with the help of bodies such as the Organisation for the Maintenance of Supplies (OMS) and the Economic League.[26] Many towns developed their voluntary organisations and, for instance, Liverpool is estimated to have had about 20,000 volunteers available of whom only about 3,400 were actually used in the dispute.[27] Haulage, which was in the hands of voluntary bodies, was organised into 150 committees. In November the government arranged to have full access to broadcasting facilities and the Ministry of Health sent out 'circular 636' to local authorities instructing them of their responsibilities under the Government's emergency provisions. By February the Home Secretary was able to inform the Cabinet that 'little remained to be done' in respect of the threatened strike.[28] The country had been divided into ten divisions and Headquarters, each with its own Civil and Road Commissioners, Coal, Finance and Food Officers appointed by the Ministry of Transport. Within these ten divisions were 150 Road Officers and the 150 Haulage Committees. Below these were a myriad of local arrangements.

The Government obviously prepared for the strike, going to the extent of moving military forces into sensitive areas, such as Liverpool, Bristol and London.[29] Yet the capacity for military involvement in strike breaking was relatively limited and much of the voluntary aspect of the preparations was more symbolic than real. The OMS, formed in August and September 1925, lacked money and was far more effective in the south of England than elsewhere. In addition, there were some disputes between the OMS and the Government based upon the former's concern to maintain independence. One such dispute occurred in Bradford in October 1925.[30] It was also clear that the OMS represented the interests of the middle and upper classes, not those of the working classes. Its President, Lord Hardinge of Penshurst, had been Viceroy of India. Its committee also included Sir J. Russell Rodd, a former British Ambassador to Italy, and Lord Jellicoe who commanded the fleet at the battle of Jutland. They were resolved to brook no opposition from the ranks despite the claim that they were a non-partisan organisation.[31] The Economic League had a wider distribution and A. McIvor has written that:

During the General Strike, the League collaborated with other employers' organisations, such as the FBI, to provide information to the government on coal stocks and shortages, the availability of transport and the organization of strike-breaking operations. Indeed, regional Leagues played an active role in strike-breaking, encouraging the enrolment of volunteer workers, providing lorry drivers, and transporting foodstuffs, and publishing news-sheets and leaflets attacking the 'pernicious influence of the reds'. In the coalfields, the district League organized a more sustained propaganda campaign, touring the colliery villages with 'flying squads', vilifying 'Cookism', supporting the Spencer brand of non-political company unionism and propagating the League's new slogan 'every man is a capitalist'.[32]

Yet it seems unlikely that the anti-Cook message would have penetrated far in the coalfields, except perhaps for the Nottingham coalfield where the Spencer union, prepared to work closely with the employers, eventually emerged.

The Government had prepared for the threatened dispute, even if weaknesses existed and persisted. In contrast, the charge levelled against the TUC is that: 'In contrast to these careful preparations on the Government side, the trade unions made virtually no effective plans for mounting a future general strike.'[33] Indeed, this charge supports Cook's reflection that 'the capitalist class in Britain, backed by a strong Tory Government, had been preparing to retrieve the position; while many of the Labour leaders, almost afraid of the growing power of Labour industrially, knowing the activities of the Government and their preparations, remained inactive'.[34] Certainly there was masterly inactivity by both the TUC and the trade union leaders, although the evidence is that this was the result of fear of defeat and the persistence of sectionalism rather than because of the prospect of success.

Walter Citrine was keenly aware of the need to prepare for conflict. The difficulty was that the unions were reluctant to relinquish their control of events to the General Council and did so only on the eve of conflict. The TUC conference, held at Scarborough between 7 and 12 September 1925, refused to give the General Council powers to call for a stoppage of work but agreed to suggest that individual unions might look to change their own rules to permit it to take action.[35] Citrine, who later became General Secretary of the TUC, attempted to puncture the complacency of the trade unions but, as with the ill-fated attempt of the miners to form an Industrial Alliance, found it difficult to obtain a broader commitment to unity. He wrote a report for the TUC's SIC suggesting the need for better and more centralised organisation and urged consultations with the Labour Party, the MFGB, the Co-operative Party and other interested bodies to force the Government into a favourable attitude. In addition he advised each union to alter their rules to give their 'Executive Council the power to declare a strike of its members in collaboration and consultation with the General Council'.[36] But little such support was forthcoming and the report was rejected by the SIC as being too extreme.

There were many meetings in which Citrine attempted to force action but little of a constructive nature took place. He acknowledged that given the economic, social and ethical problems it would pose 'A general strike, therefore, is a literal impossibility . . .'.[37] His own doubts were amplified by the lack of trust which emerged when the SIC met the MFGB on 24 February 1926: 'I could see immediately Thomas spoke that the miners were on the alert. It seemed to me that they were looking for something, expecting to find that Thomas was trying to trick them.'[38] J. Ramsay MacDonald later emphasised the point to Citrine that 'Jimmy is one of the most loyal men in the world, but I'm afraid the miners don't see eye to eye with him.'[39] Thomas' reputation amongst the miners was conditioned by his 'betrayal' of them on 'Black Friday', and was not helped by his quick rebuke of Cook's preparations. Cook had dismissed the threat of troops by stating that 'bayonets can't cut coal' . . . 'We have already beaten not only the employers, but the strongest Government in modern times', and adding that 'My own mother-in-law has been taking in an extra tin of salmon for weeks past . . .'. Thomas retorted: 'By God! A British revolution based on a tin of salmon.'[40] The hurt was even greater when Cook began to realise the SIC would have to rely upon the support of the General Council and Thomas, whom the miners vilified as a master of intrigue. In such a situation of animosity and distrust, the trade unions failed to take positive action until the last possible moment. Indeed, Ernest Bevin verified this point to a Conference of Executives (of unions) in January 1927:

With regard to the preparation for the strike, there were no preparations until April, 27 (1926), and I do not want anyone to go
away from this conference under the impression that the General
Council had any particular plan to run the movement. In fact the
General Council did not sit down to draft the plans until they were
called together on April 27th, and it is better for everybody to know
the task was thrown upon us from April 27th to May 1st, and when
that task is understood you will be able to appreciate, not the little
difficulties, but the wonderful response and organization we
had.[41]

In the final analysis, the Government had prepared for action
whilst the TUC had not. Yet, despite their contrasting strategies
both pinned their hopes on the possibility that the Samuel Commission might somehow achieve a compromise between the two
main intransigent groups, the coal owners and the coal miners.

The Samuel Commission

The Royal Commission on the Coal Industry (1925), better known
as the Samuel Commission, was officially formed on 5 September
1925 to examine the coal industry in its widest sense, touching
upon the need for rationalisation, the possible nationalising of
coal royalties, and the issue of wage levels. Its brief was 'To
inquire into and report upon the economic position of the Coal
Industry and the conditions affecting it and to make any recommendations for the improvement thereof.'[42] It was to be an independent body and so three of its four members were Liberals: Sir
Herbert Samuel, the wartime Home Secretary and ex-Governor
of Palestine; Kenneth Lee, a textile manufacturer; and W. H.
Beveridge, Director of the London School of Economics. The
fourth member was Sir Herbert Lawrence. In addition, both sides
of the coal industry were allowed to appoint assessors, five in all,
who had the right to take part in the examination of witnesses.
However, its very independence made it a maverick to the
interests of all the parties involved, except the TUC. Its recommendations, published in March 1926, had no chance of settling
the mining dispute.

The Samuel Commission Report rejected the idea of
nationalising the coal industry and mainly focused upon ways in
which the coal industry could be reorganised. Amongst its many

recommendations were the need to amalgamate existing mines, to nationalise mining royalties, to increase research into coal production and to improve industrial relations. The last objective, it was maintained, might be achieved by a cocktail of measures including the development of profit-sharing schemes, the formation of pit committees, the introduction of a family allowance system, and the maintenance of national wage agreements with some regional variations.[43] It acknowledged that such changes would take years and in the immediate future the way forward was not to extend hours or to continue the subsidy, which was 'indefensible' and 'should never be repeated', but to reduce the minimum wages of the miners.[44] These policies embarrassed the Government, offended the miners and aggrieved the mine owners.

The Government opposed the nationalisation of mining royalties as being too expensive, and was reluctant to mount a campaign for reorganisation of the industry but suggested that it would agree to the Samuel Report if both coal owners and coal miners would accept it. There was little chance of that. The majority of employers opposed national wage settlements and were reluctant to consider the rationalisation of coal mines, which they claimed had already been going on. The miners simply refused to accept wage reductions. Indeed, both A. J. Cook and Herbert Smith had counted out such a suggestion in giving evidence before the Samuel Commission and often repeated their famous dictum 'Not a penny off the pay, not a second on the day.' The fact was, as A. J. Cook remarked for the MFGB, that the Samuel Commission 'gives us threequarters, and we can't accept it'.[45] Smith added that 'I want to see the horse I am going to mount.'[46] The miners had three basic demands – national wage agreements, the seven-hour day, and no wage reductions – all of which were anathema to the mine-owners. Between the miners and the mine owners there was a wide gulf which was never likely to be bridged by even the most protracted negotiations.

In the face of such intransigent opposition to the Samuel Report by the two main sides, the TUC's general approval seems to lack any sense of reality. Thomas welcomed the Samuel Report as 'a wonderful document'.[47] Citrine, and the other leading lights of the TUC, saw it as a basis for settlement. The fact is that they scented defeat if a settlement was not reached. In a chat with Ramsay MacDonald and Arthur Pugh, on 9 March 1926, the day before the publication of the Samuel Report, Citrine reflected that:

> During the conversation we fell to talking about the possibilities of our being defeated in the forthcoming struggle which seems inevitable in the mining industry. We were all agreed that we should avoid a clash if we possibly could.[48]

Indeed, there was a fatalism about the TUC's need to negotiate. It promoted negotiations on the terms of the Samuel Commission throughout March and April 1926, knowing full well that they could only succeed in the unlikely event of the miners accepting wage reductions. There was never the remotest chance that that was going to occur.

Negotiations

On the 24 March Baldwin informed the House of Commons that the Samuel Commission contained some proposals to which he was opposed but that he would consider them if both sides of the industry would accept its recommendations. The Government then withdrew and for about a month a flurry of negotiations occurred between the owners and miners, with the TUC attempting to mediate. The efforts at finding agreement proved futile. The meetings became bogged down with debates about minimum wages for the different mining districts, guaranteed weeks and the minutia of wage arrangements. The very fact that talks took place at all was due to the willingness of Cook, if not Smith, to tinker with the MFGB's three basic demands.[49] But the sticking point came on the 12 and 13 April when the Mining Association refused to even contemplate the need for a minimum national wage. The miners decided not to continue negotiations and the individual coal owners in the Mining Association began to issue their new wage rates and invited the coal miners to have district talks. The Mining Association eventually informed the Prime Minister of their, harsh, wage conditions for each district on 21 April.

The MFGB had already recognised the need to strengthen TUC support. On 26 February the miners had obtained from the SIC a commitment that 'There was to be no reduction in wages, no increase in working hours, and no interference with the principle of national agreements.'[50] Cook, and other miner's leaders, latched on to this statement when condemning both the TUC's pusillanimous attitude revealed in its last-minute attempts to avert the General Strike and its eventual decision to call the strike off. However, Phillips suggests that this statement was something of an interim position, adopted until the Samuel *Report* was published and that, as John Bromley suggested, the SIC were only 'agreeing to defend those principles so far as they could, and it would not debar the miners from making concessions in the course of negotiations'.[51] The miners' representatives might well have suspected the equivocal attitude of the SIC when it met with it on 8, 14, 23 April. This uncertainty about the TUC appears to have surfaced on 23 April when Herbert Smith asked 'Was the General Council prepared to say that the miners ought to submit to a reduction in wages?' Arthur Pugh replied by suggesting that the SIC 'wanted to proceed on the basis of no reductions but they must see what that would involve on Government and everybody else'.[52] In other words the SIC held an ambiguous attitude towards the impending dispute, clearly hoping that a settlement could be effected to avoid industrial conflict.

The TUC, through the SIC, played an important but subordinate role in the events which led up to the General Strike. The problem it faced was developing a policy and strategy which would enable it to avoid having to implement its vague, and equivocal, commitment to supporting the miners whilst at the same time avoiding a charge of betrayal. It was an impossible tightrope to walk. Nevertheless, on 8 April Arthur Pugh maintained that that there was a need to reorganise the coal industry and during the next two weeks there emanated from the TUC numerous schemes for joint boards and the like. On 13 April Walter Citrine urged the SIC to prepare recommendations for a settlement and join the miners in negotiations. However, the SIC did not meet with the miners in joint negotiations until 26 April, at which point several unions were already making arrangements for strike pay. Even then, the decision to have the miners and the SIC join together in negotiations was taken by Baldwin rather than the TUC. Yet, from that moment onwards the SIC acted to shape events. The matter of a policy was considered by the General Council on 27 April and two days later, a joint committee of the TUC and the miners produced *The Mining Situation*, which was laid before the General Council and the miners. This accepted the need to reorganise and rationalise the coal industry but rejected the need to reduce wages or abrogate 'the present standard of hours'.[53] This policy statement was outlined at a conference of trade union executives held at Memorial Hall on the morning of 29 April 1926, where Pugh also referred to Baldwin's recent intervention in the dispute.

The TUC hoped that the Government would intervene in the dispute but, despite several meetings between the TUC and the Government and the miners and the Government, this did not occur until 23 April. What triggered it was the fact that the previous day the MFGB had rejected the harsh wage reductions being imposed by the Mining Association and an *impasse* had been reached. Therefore, Baldwin re-entered the fray and explored the possibility of getting the owners to establish a reasonably high national minimum wage along with the reinstatement of a longer working day.

On Sunday, 25 April Baldwin invited the TUC Chairman, Arthur Pugh, to a secret meeting at Chequers to discuss the crisis in an informal manner. At this meeting, Pugh expressed the view that too much attention had been focused upon wages and not enough on reoganisation.[54] The next day, Baldwin met the SIC and suggested the same to them, inviting them, as already indicated, to depute one or two representatives to accompany the miners' representatives in discussion.[55] Yet there was little scope for negotiation and matters soon became bogged down. Baldwin, if asked to arbitrate, was intending to maintain existing wages for another two years and to extend the hours of work. He said as much to Evan Williams of the Mining Association, but his ideas were rejected by the mine owners. The only thing they would consider was the possibility of a low minimum national wage which, of course, the miners would not accept.

The final efforts at settlement

On Thursday 29 April, the eve of the threatened coal lock-out, more than 800 delegates, representing the executives of 141 trade unions affiliated to the TUC, met at Memorial Hall, Farringdon Street, London. The policy of the TUC and the MFGB, presented in *The Mining Situation* was put to them and Bevin suggested that, given the unpromising situation, 'In twenty-four hours from now you have to cease being separate unions. For this purpose you will have to become one union with no autonomy.'[56] Subsequently, there was a vote to give the General Council the responsibility for conducting the dispute and calling a strike if necessary. The SIC, which now became the Negotiating Committee, then took up the responsibility of attempting to settle the dispute and went to the House of Commons where they met Baldwin just after midnight. He promised to pass on the coal owners' offer the next morning. The harsh terms, already referred to, were received the following afternoon and were immediately summarily rejected by the miners' delegate conference. There followed a number of feverish negotiations.

On that evening, of the 30 April, the miners' executive and the Negotiating Committee, along with Arthur Henderson and Ramsay MacDonald, pressured Baldwin to get the lock-out notices suspended. During a tetchy four-hour meeting, Thomas produced a copy of an OMS poster announcing the proclamation of a State of Emergency. According to Citrine:

> Jimmy Thomas looked the Prime Minister straight in the eye and asked him had this poster been ordered by the Government and did it represent the mind of the Government? Baldwin flushed and then, after a few seconds hesitation, said that it was true that the Government had taken the necessary steps to prepare for the proclamation of a state of emergency, but the poster had not yet been published. The silence was ominous. Every one of us concluded that we had been badly tricked. We felt that we could no longer trust Baldwin or anyone else and that they were simply playing for time to complete the arrangements which the Government had in hand.[57]

Trust evaporated immediately and the trade union delegation returned to Memorial Hall where Pugh gave a factual account of the day's proceedings. The general secretaries of the various unions were then taken to a nearby room and each handed a copy of the 'Proposals for Co-ordinated Action'.[58] It stated that work would cease entirely in transport, printing, iron and steel, metal and heavy chemical industries at a time still to be specified by the General Council. The builders were also to down tools on work other than hospitals. Yet health and sanitary arrangements were to be maintained. The concern of the document was to exert the maximum impact of the strike without causing danger and inconvenience to the public. Orderly activity was to be to the fore, with violence against property and riots to be avoided.

On the following day, Saturday 1 May, union executives met separately to consider the proposals and then gathered in Memorial Hall to vote on them. Thomas attempted to get the National Union of Railwaymen to keep out of the dispute but was overruled by his executive. At noon the vote was taken and the the General Council was given the powers to run the impending stoppage, by 3,653,577 votes to 49,911.[59] From that point, the whole of the trade union movement and the miners had surrendered responsibility for running the dispute to the General Council. The TUC was also committed to securing the withdrawal of lock-out notices before negotiations could be reopened. The course was now set fair for the General Strike to begin at a minute to midnight on 3 May 1926.

The TUC had been propelled forward into a conflict which it had always sought to avoid and therefore, despite the limitations under which it operated, sought to have talks about the re-opening of talks. On 1 May it informed the Government, in two letters, that it would work to maintain essential services, not wishing to alienate the public and hold itself available for further talks. It was hoped that the miners, who had not officially disowned the Samuel *Report*, might be persuaded into some type of compromise arrangement. Baldwin proposed that a sub-committee of four members from each side, the TUC and the Government, should meet and discuss the dispute, without record. The Negotiating Committee chose Pugh, Thomas, Swales and Citrine to meet with Baldwin, Birkenhead, Steel-Maitland and Horace Wilson. Debarred from negotiating without the withdrawal of lock-out notices the sub-committee was diverted towards discussing how a public subsidy might be temporarily renewed for a couple of weeks and a return to work secured. The two sections of the sub-committee sat in different rooms with Horace Wilson as the intermediary and the TUC appears to have had some ill-founded confidence that the Samuel *Report* might yet form the basis of a settlement. Thomas favoured an acceptance of the *Report* and felt that a settlement could be arranged within a fortnight. Other TUC negotiators clung to similar hopes.

Yet when they reported back to the full General Council on 2 May, their hopes were dashed by the miners' leaders who declined to accept the suggestion. According to Cook, the miners' leaders were stung by the insouciant behaviour of the Negotiating Committee in meeting the Government in secret 'in spite of their pledge to the miners only to negotiate with them'.[60]

Yet the General Council persisted with this formula for settlement and instructed the Negotiating Committee to find out more details of the Government's intentions. But the Government was less than happy with the arrangements, feeling that they were vague and did not ensure a successful outcome. It would not contemplate even a very short-term subsidy without the withdrawal of the threat of a general strike. During the afternoon, Baldwin and his ministers prepared an ultimatum to the TUC and the miners to accept interim adjustments to hours or wages and the unconditional withdrawal of the threat of a general strike prior to negotiations and reorganisation.

The General Council's representatives went to Downing Street at 9pm on 2 May but the meeting with the Government was unrewarding. The General Council could not guarantee a settlement and the Government, offering what became known as the 'Birkenhead formula', demanded that the miners must concede on hours or pay whilst reorganisation was under way. This quickly proved to be a non-starter for both sides and was already dead as an issue by the time the miners' executive arrived at Downing Street at 11.15pm. By that time the formula of the previous night, a settlement within two weeks based upon the Samuel *Report*, was being floated again. But to avoid being bogged down, Bevin suggested that there should be an independent wages board which would be responsible for ensuring that reorganisation took place in advance of adjudicating wage rates. This board would recommend and approve the legislation necessary for reorganisation, and the Government, the mine owners and miners would accept its decisions.[61] But this did not get very far because the Cabinet ultimatum, mentioned above, effectively ended negotiations. These were already faltering once the Government realised that trade unions were sending telegrams to their members finalising arrangements for the strike. The imbroglio was ended by the refusal of the *Daily Mail* printers in London to set up the 'For King and Country' editorial on the threatened strike. It was the final pretext for calling off the attempts to find grounds for negotiations.

The *Daily Mail* incident is infamous in the folklore of Labour history. It appears that the Cabinet was already moving to ending negotiations, due to pressure from its right wingers, when the news of the cessation of work at the *Daily Mail* came through. In the early morning of the 3 May, some authorities say at 12.45 and others at 1.15am, Pugh, Thomas, Swales and Citrine were called out of discussions between the General Council and the miners to meet Baldwin who handed them a note which referred to 'overt acts . . . including interference with the freedom of the Press' as grounds for ending the talks. The TUC representatives then went next door to their colleagues and then on to their colleagues at Eccleston Square. There they prepared a reply disowning the printers' strike and deploring the curtailment of negotiations. They also appointed a sub-committee of Bevin, Pugh, Citrine, Smith, Richardson and Cook, to complete the outline agreements which were being discussed when the Government called an end to negotiations, Baldwin having retired to bed. The next day they and the miners agreed to a statement about the need to reorganise the coal industry through a wages board and then to discuss wages.

The break in direct negotiations occurred with less than twenty-four hours to the start of the General Strike. Although there were no direct negotiations on 3 May Ramsay MacDonald sought to intervene, raising the matter in the House of Commons and subsequently attempting to get Baldwin to take action to avert the coming conflict. He and Arthur Henderson got short shrift in their meeting with Baldwin and Government ministers. Citrine, recording the incident second hand, wrote:

> It appears from what Henderson told me that Churchill was going to prove that we could not dictate to the Government . . .
> Henderson retorted 'It seems to me Winston that you are trying to give us a dose of Sidney Street.'
> Churchill replied, 'You will be better prepared to talk to us in two or three weeks.'[62]

Immediately after this meeting the Government issued its statement about the impending strike, which was published in the press on 3 May. It referred to its commitment to the Samuel

Commission and its willingness to to provide a two-week subsidy during which negotiations could be continued, but stressed that it abhorred the 'gross interference' with the freedom of the press since 'such action involves the challenge to the constitutional right and freedom of the nation'. It declared that:

> His Majesty's Government, therefore, before they can continue negotiations, must require from the Trade Union Committee both the repudiation of the actions referred to as having already taken place, and the immediate unconditional withdrawal of the instructions for a general strike.[63]

The General Council did repudiate the strike at the *Daily Mail* but there was no immediate prospect that it would withdraw the threat of a general strike. The Government would not budge and the nation drifted into industrial conflict.

Conclusion

On the coming of the General Strike, Citrine wrote in his diary, on 2 May, that 'We had a vision of 1921 in our minds.'[64] This is a telling comment which Phillips makes much of in his book on the subject, capturing as it does the desire not to repeat 'Black Friday'. This, and the evidence presented, would suggest that the TUC had little option but to intervene to help the miners, however reluctant they were to do so. They acknowledged that something had to be done to defend the miners against wage cuts as a strategy against further reductions in other industries. Even the attempts of Jimmy Thomas to avert the strike failed to stem the tidal flow of support for the miners' case. Nevertheless, it is clear that the TUC had no stomach for what was to come. Citrine feared the worst as he attempted to force a reluctant TUC to prepare for action but, as Bevin said, it was not until the 27 April that the TUC took the situation seriously.

What explains this masterful inactivity? The answer would appear to be a complex weave of tensions and fears. On the one hand, there was distrust between the miners and the TUC, based largely upon the miners' fear, largely justified, that Thomas was involved in intrigue against their interests. Such divisive concern and hostility pours out of Cook's pamphlet *The Nine Days*. Secondly, the TUC and the main unions were reluctant to prepare for a conflict which they did not desire and could not win. Because of these concerns and tensions, and the hamstrung nature of any action the TUC could take, it drifted into the dispute ill-prepared and with no clear policy or strategy. It could see that victory for the trade unions against a powerful and prepared Government was simply unrealistic. It therefore latched on to the Samuel Commission as the medium for compromise. However, the coal-owners were unwilling to contemplate the need for reorganisation until wage reductions and longer hours were conceded by the miners. On the other hand, the miners were resolute in their demands that wages would not be cut, that hours would not be increased and that national negotiations would not be abandoned. All the negotiations which occurred were riddled with vague generalities and consequent misunderstandings, which arose out of the desire to bridge what proved to be an unbridgeable chasm between the coal-owners and the coal-miners. In the final analysis, there was almost no prospect that the Samuel Commission could ever resolve the problems which had developed in mining over the previous ten, if not fifty, years. There was always a possibility that the General Strike could have been avoided, but that seemed increasingly remote in the early months of 1926. The ingredients necessary for conflict had conflated in 1925 in such a way as to ensure that the TUC was forced to help the miners, the Government could not back down again, and that the TUC would thrash around and support any pretext for settling the dispute. Phillips, rightly and tellingly comments that 'If the TUC fought the General Strike with little semblance of purpose, the government fought it with none at all. . . .'.[65] The Government and the TUC proved incapable of settling a dispute between two intractable opponents.

On 2 and 3 May 1926 any control the TUC had over events disappeared once the Government suspended negotiations. For the next nine days it was faced with demonstrating that it could organise a national conflict and force both Government and employers to recognise that even the symbolic action of supporting the miners could be extremely damaging to their interests. This may have been the long-term result of the General Strike but what is clear in the short term is that there was a gallant, if uneven, response to the strike call amongst the trade unions and workers of Britain.

Notes

1 Citrine, 'Mining Crisis and National Strike'.
2 *Ibid.*, 10 July 1925.
3 W. Citrine, *Men and Work*, Hutchinson, London, 1964, pp. 133–4.
4 *Macmillan Inquiry Report*, HMSO, London, 1925, p. 19.
5 Phillips, *General Strike*, p. 54.
6 Citrine, 'Mining Crisis and National Strike', 27 July 1925, p. 27.
7 Citrine, *Men and Work*, p. 139.
8 Citrine, 'Mining Crisis and National Strike', pp. 32–3.
9 Cab 23/50/27/25, 28 May 1925.
10 Cab 27/259, CP 356 (25).
11 TUC *Report*, 1925, pp. 179–80.
12 Cab 23/50 42 (25).
13 Symons, *General Strike*, pp. 23–4.
14 Phillips, *General Strike*, p. 65; Cab 23/50 42 (25).
15 Renshaw, *General Strike*, pp. 125–7.
16 Quoted in Tom Bell, *The British Communist Party: a Short History*, London, 1927, p. 109.
17 *The Times*, 24 August 1925; *Lansbury's Labour Weekly*, 8 August 1925.
18 MFGB, *Annual Delegate Conference* (1925), quoted in Bullock, *Bevin*, p. 281.
19 TUC *Report*, 1925, p. 183; *The Mining Dispute*, p. 3.
20 *Hansard*, 187, cs 1605–12.
21 Crook, *General Strike*, p. 294, quoting *The Nation*, New York.
22 Citrine. 'Mining Crisis and National Strike', introduction, p. 3.
23 *Labour Magazine*, September 1925, pp. 195–6.
24 *The Times*, 3 August 1925.
25 A. Mason, 'The Government and the General Strike', *International Review of Social History*, 14, 1968.
26 A. M. McIvor, 'Essay in Anti-Labour History', *Society for the Study of Labour History, Bulletin*, 53, 1, 1988.
27 Baines and Bean, 'Merseyside', p. 254.
28 Cab 81 (26).
29 Disposition of Fleet, 16 May 1926, PRO Adm 1/8697; for troop dispositions look at WO 73/123. A map of the distribution of armed forces is provided in J. Foster, 'British Imperialism', p. 47. A battleship/cruiser and four other ships were placed off Liverpool, there were two battleships and three other ships in the Bristol Channel, four battleships/cruisers and 20 other ships in the Thames, and ships and troops in many other centres.
30 Phillips, *General Strike*, p. 97.
31 *The Times*, 6 October 1925.

32 McIvor, 'Anti-Labour History', p. 1.

33 Renshaw, *General Strike*, p. 134.

34 A. J. Cook, *The Nine Days: The Story of the General Strike told by the Miners' Secretary*, London, Miners' Women and Children Fund, 1926, p. 3.

35 *Labour Gazette*, September 1925.

36 Citrine, *Men and Work*, pp. 144, 146–7, 151–2.

37 Citrine, 'Mining Crisis and National Strike', 4 January 1926.

38 *Ibid.*, 24 February 1926.

39 *Ibid.*, 3 March 1926.

40 J. H. Thomas, *My Story*, London, 1937, pp. 105–6.

41 TUC General Council, *Report of Proceedings at a Special Conference of Executives*, 20 January 1927. Also quoted in Crook, *General Strike*, pp. 311–12 and many other books on the subject.

42 *Report on the Royal Commission on the Coal Industry (1925), Report*, HMSO, Cmd 2600, 1926, p. xi.

43 *Ibid.*, pp. 232–5.

44 *Ibid.*, pp.235–7.

45 Davies, *Cook*, p. 91.

46 Minutes of a Meeting Between the Mining Association and the MFGB, 26 March 1926, BP, D.3, 13, pp. 223–55.

47 Davies, *Cook*, p. 92.

48 Citrine, 'Mining Crisis and the National Strike', p. 131.

49 Davies, *Cook*, pp. 94–5.

50 Cook, *Nine Days*, p. 4.

51 Phillips, *General Strike*, pp.88–9, quoting GC 123 13/6/131, SIC, 26 February 1926.

52 SIC, 23 April; TU Conference of Executives, 29 April 1926.

53 TUC, *The Mining Situation*, TUC, London, 1926, paras. 4, 6, 9, 11, 12, 15.

54 T. Jones, *Whitehall Dairies* II, 1926–1930, Oxford University Press, London, 1969, ed. by K. Middlemass, p. 22.

55 Cab 27/3/7 ROC 26/16, p. 5, 26 April 1926.

56 Report of Special Conference of Trade Union Executives, 29 April–1 May 1926. Also quoted in Farman, *General Strike*, p. 91.

57 Citrine, 'Mining Crisis and National Strike', p. 162.

58 Look at the Document Section.

59 TU Conference of Executives, *Report*, 1 May 1926, p. 33.

60 Cook, *Nine Days*, p. 16.

61 Bevin Series Box 3, C2/2 15 and 16.

62 Citrine, 'Mining Crisis and National Strike', p. 218.

63 Government statement issued to the newspapers. Look at the Document Section.

64 Citrine, 'Mining Crisis and National Strike, p. 185.

65 Phillips, *General Strike*, p. 133.

3

'The wonderful response and the organisation we had': the Nine Days

Ernest Bevin reflected upon 'the wonderful response and organisation we had' during the General Strike, given that the TUC made no effective attempt to make preparations until 27 April.[1] At the other political extreme of the trade union spectrum, A. J. Cook wrote that 'Tuesday, May 4th, started with the workers answering the call. What a wonderful response! What loyalty! What solidarity! From John O'Groats to Land's End the workers answered the call to arms to defend us, to defend the brave miner in his fight for a living wage.'[2] Yet such agreement hides a world of differences between the right and the left of the trade union movement and it should be remembered that Cook felt that the rank and file acted better than their leaders, whom he considered to be bereft of both principle and policy. Other contemporaries were less convinced of the magnificence of the response. Emile Burns applauded the enthusiasm of the rank and file but derided the haphazard nature of preparations and organisation, which meant that many councils of action and strike committees were not formed until the eve of the dispute.[3] So how effective was the trade union response to the General Strike?

In order to measure the the strike response it is vital to examine the preparation and organisation of both the TUC and the Government. A number of questions arise from such an examination. First, how effective was the TUC in maintaining support for the strike? Secondly, and conversely, how effective was the Government in dealing with this unprecedented strike situation, the most outstanding event in British industrial relations? Indeed, thirdly, how seriously did the Government take the constitutional threat posed by the dispute and what was its strategy? Apart from these questions relating to the national situation it is also necessary to assess the local pattern of events. For instance, how did the Government's local network of control hold up to the challenge of the trade unions? How effective was the control of the trade unionists – did it vary considerably from region to region?

On the whole, the national area of debate is rather easier to examine than the local situation and evidence suggest that the General Council developed reasonably effective administrative machinery – performing quite impressively despite its lack of communication and the consequent confusion that arose over the role of trades councils, strike committees and transport com- mittees – even though there was never any serious challenge to Government hegemony. The local events are more difficult to analyse, for although there were upwards of twenty local studies produced by the mid-1970s, some of them very brief indeed, there have only been a handful of local studies published since then.[4] Although these studies are immensely varied in the regions they examine, and the approach they take, they tend, by and large, to agree in presenting the General Strike as a chaotic, even if heroic, attempt to support the miners. But they can never offer more than a limited and partial report on the areas, which, by and large, were reasonably well organised during the dispute. Also, the local dimension raises many related questions. How effective were local strike organisations? How did the authorities respond? Were there many volunteers? Was there much violence? Did the Communist Party exert any significant influence?

The General Council and its conduct of the dispute

Between 1,500,000 and 1,750,000 workers came out on strike on 4 May in support of one million miners who were locked out and and stayed out for nine days. Most of these were the first line workers employed in transport, printing, iron and steel, power stations, building and the chemical industries. The second line workers, employed in industries such as engineering, shipbuilding and textiles, were held in reserve. Of these, only the engineers and shipbuilding workers were called out as from 12 May, the day the General Strike ended. To bring out so many workers was a major feat and from the start the General Council attempted to create an administrative structure commensurate with the task of organisation it faced. Bevin and the Ways and Means Committee, soon to become the Powers and Orders Committee, co-ordinated the activities of the various unions, and the Food and Essential Services Committee was formed to make arrangements for the distribution of food and the maintenance of the health services. There was a Publicity Committee, formed to counter Government propaganda, and another one, headed by Margaret Bondfield, which, rather belatedly, decided that only local transport committees, based upon the transport unions, would be able to issue permits for the distribution of food. Although hastily contrived the TUC's administrative structure worked tolerably well, within the confines of what the Government allowed.

Much of the credit for this success must go to Ernest Bevin who, with the Strike Organisation Committee (formerly the Powers and Orders Committee), exercised overall responsibility for the conduct of the dispute. Although his control of the situation was somewhat febrile at the beginning of the dispute it gradually extended throughout many essential industries. For instance, in the electricity industry Bevin, and his committee, could claim that it had secured ten agreements to cut off industrial power in London and to have withdrawn the labour from 18 out of 22 municipal undertakings and 19 of 31 private concerns by 10 May. As Bevin reflected, such success might depend upon 'not having too may generals in the business'.[5] But whilst the Strike Organisation Committee could shape the overall direction of policy there was no way in which it could maintain more than symbolic control of the myriad of activities which fell within its compass. There had been no other dispute on the scale of the General Strike and one should not expect too much of the TUC's administrative structure. Indeed, all it could do was to act in an expedient manner and smooth out the problems as they arose.

From the start TUC control was riddled with problems. The most immediate one was that of permits. The TUC agreed that their issue should be co-ordinated through the NUR headquarters at Euston Road but, on 6 May, because of problems of inconsistency of treatment it was decided that they should all be reviewed by local transport committees. This was difficult since most councils of action had assumed that they had the right to issue them to allow the movement of goods or to agree to strikers remaining at work. In the case of Bradford, for instance, the permits read as follows: Miners' Lockout 1926. Emergency Committee. This is to certify that . . . has received sanction to. . . . Signed on behalf of the Emergency Committee, Walter Barber, Secretary.[6]

Mindful of this confusion the National Transport Committee, consisting of all the transport unions, circulated telegrams to all the local transport committees on 7 May. The following was sent to Liverpool:

7.15 PM LONDON CTO
EDWARDS ENGINEERS HALL MOUNT PLEASANT LV
WE INSTRUCT ALL LOCAL TRANSPORT COMMITTEES REVIEW ALL PERMITS WHICH HAVE BEEN ISSUED NO TRADES COUNCIL LABOUR PARTY COUNCIL OF ACTION STRIKE COMMITTEE OR TRADE UNION BRANCH HAS AUTHORITY TO DEAL WITH PERMITS PLEASE CONVEY TO ALL CONCERNED + NATIONAL TRANSPORT COMMITTEE UNITY HOUSE LONDON[7]

The telegrams clarified the issue but did little to solve the problem. A plethora of permits existed in many towns. This situation was noted by the *Workers' Chronicle*, issued by G. H. Laraman for the Newcastle Trades Council of Action, which commented that:

IS TOFFEE FOOD
Comrades & fellow Workers
    The question of the moment is who can handle food supplies. It is the most important question of today. Will the machinery break (ask Sir Kingsley Wood). He asks the workers to handle it, and next moment claims all is O.K. . . .
    It's all very well from a publicity point of view to see all vehicles marked food supplies, but in all my experience as Organiser in one of the main Food Trades I never knew Dainty Toffee, Ice Cream etc. could be called food unless there was a surplus of labels to use up.[8]

The TUC never had control of the issue of permits and its influence over other activities was severely circumscribed by the Government's emergency measures. Many of the London power stations still operated, although sometimes with TUC approval, and a similar pattern was repeated throughout the country. For instance, at Barnsley power station, in the heart of the important Yorkshire coalfield, the work continued and the power workers lived in the station throughout the strike.[9] At a number of ports work continued with the help of volunteers even if other groups of workers had come out. On Merseyside, for instance, out of ninety-two ships of over 1,000 tons in ports on 4 May, twenty-five had left by 15 May and fifty more had arrived.[10] And in Dover, volunteers kept the port working.[11] The propaganda and publicity aspect of the TUC's work was also restricted. The Government ensured that the 'independent' BBC would not allow trade unionists or their sympathisers to broadcast. The newsprint of the *Daily Herald* was largely confiscated by the Government, thus restricting output of the *British Worker*, the newspaper of the TUC which, in London, was edited by Hamilton Fyfe, editor of the *Daily Herald*. Although the *British Worker* went into production on 5 May, and was distributed by print workers through trade unions, its circulation of around 500,000 did not meet demand and the other editions produced in Glasgow, Cardiff, Newcastle, Sunderland, Leicester and Leeds failed to make good the deficiency.[12]

The TUC also failed to strengthen its connections with organisations which could have improved the effectiveness of the strike. In particular, its relations with the co-operative movement left much to be desired. On the eve of the strike the Co-operative Union was requesting some form of indemnification from losses through the security of trade union funds, but the TUC was not in a position to offer such a guarantee. This offence was compounded by the fact that the TUC gave no special dispensations or privileges to the co-operative movement throughout the dispute. However, despite these frosty relationships many local co-operatives were supportive of the General Strike.[13]

Summarising the situation, it is obvious that the strike organisation of the TUC left a great deal to be desired. It was hastily contrived to meet a situation which had never occurred before. As a result it combined the faults of expediency with those derived from exploring a new landscape for industrial relations. The lack of a developed trade union alliance was a major problem. In contrast, the Government had prepared carefully for all contingencies.

The Government: objectives and preparations

Stanley Baldwin, the Prime Minister, was a life-long advocate of industrial peace and believed that he could bring the coal owners and the coalminers together to avoid conflict. Yet within his Cabinet there were hardliners who were less sanguine about treating with trade unionists, just as there was elsewhere within the Conservative Party. Baldwin's position was further weakened by his decision to provide a subsidy for the coal industry in July 1925, not least because of a Tory press campaign which was generally hostile to his decision. Therefore, Baldwin approached the General Strike hoping for industrial peace but resolved, and prepared, to face the strike if need be. Above all, he believed that the coal industry, like other industries, had to settle its own problems and that the Government could not be expected to provide a further subsidy, at least not one for more than a couple of weeks. To the Government, the Samuel Commission, and its policy of industrial reorganisation, combined with both changes in the hours of work and the level of pay, offered the best prospect of dealing with the current and future problems of the coal industry. Thus the Government's policy strongly favoured rationalisation rather than a subsidy. A General Strike aimed at coercing the Government into changing this policy was, therefore, deemed to be unconstitutional and a challenge to parliamentary democracy. Threatened with a General Strike with such an objective it is clear that the Government could not negotiate with the TUC or the miners. It therefore remained for it to ensure that it maintained control of the nation throughout the crisis.

The Government had two main priorities in conducting the strike. The first was to maintain food supplies, and vital services, and the second to preserve law and order. Generally, it achieved both objectives throughout most of the country, despite the strength of trade union grass-root support.

It began to issue its emergency proclamations at the beginning of the coal lock-out. Thereafter, the operation of its emergency activities proved impressively smooth. It issued the Ministry of Health Circular 703 on 5 May to instruct the Board of Guardians

not to provide relief to strikers. It maintained its strike organisation throughout the country and found that it had no need to
draw upon many of the estimated 300,000 to 500,000 volunteers
at its disposal. Most areas had 20,000 or more volunteers, far
more than was required for the crisis, and in London, where
114,000 men had come forward by 11 May only 9,500 had been
given work.[14] The OMS and other voluntary groups supplying
the Government with labour were hardly in demand, although
2,000 Cambridge undergraduates were called up to work on the
underground, in power stations, as special constables, and on
the docks The fact is that the Government was able to maintain
the operation of road transport because the haulage committees
were always able to rely upon regular drivers. It was regular
drivers and temporary recruits who kept the special convoys
moving to the docks and the Hyde Park milk scheme centre
throughout the dispute. Indeed, the Government's transport and
maintenance of food distribution became so effective that by the
end of the General Strike co-operative societies, nominally recognised to be in the TUC camp, were asking divisional food officers
to provide volunteers, transport and police protection in certain
instances.[15]

The docks were vital to Government control of food supplies.
Volunteer labour was moved into many docks, such as Liverpool,
Bristol, Cardiff, Glasgow, Leith and Dover. A rare insight into
how effectively organised this was is offered by a Henry
Duckworth, one of the 460 Cambridge undergraduates who
worked on the docks, and one of the chief organisers of the
'Dover Dockers', better known as the 'Dover Fifty', who acted as
strike-breakers throughout the dispute.[16]

On the 4 May, Duckworth, having failed to organise all the
Trinity College men into a volunteer force, decided to organise a
sampling of 'all the fittest and ablest in Cambridge'.[17] On
Thursday 6 May he and these fellow undergraduates proceeded
to travel from Cambridge to Dover. And what an ostentatious
show of class conflict it was: 'Birkin, our chauffeur, plus a guard
for the return journey, was ordered to be round at Great Gate
with his 100 m.p.h. Bentley at five o'clock. . . . Birkin had
removed his windscreen in case he should have a brickback
thrown at him . . . since he was not actually a member of the
so-called "Dover Fifty".'[18]

Thereafter, Duckworth offers a lengthy description of the living quarters, the arrangements and the events surrounding the 97 students who worked for Southern Railway in the Dover docks, loading and unloading passenger liners, cargo boats and the like. Apparently, there was only one skilled blackleg:

> . . . Fletcher by name. . . . He was a pleasant fellow eager to do well so as to get taken on by the SR when the strike was over. He had been dismissed by the Company, so rumour has it, for being mixed up in a theft which took place in the hold of a ship. The party of blackleg casual labour was composed of all the riff-raff of the town, who adopted a ca-canny policy as regards work of any kind.[19]

Fletcher and a Home Office officer named Wilkins were the only ones who knew how to operate the cranes.

Duckworth's diary suggests that all the skilled and semi-skilled workers who normally worked for the Southern Railway and on the docks were out. The docks were picketed, there was a great deal of talk about threats and violence, night guard was kept, some of the blackleg casuals were beaten up and special constables were put on guard. There was a public schoolboy feel to the whole affair, one which must have heightened class an industrial tensions by the fact that the chauffeurs became involved in the dispute:

> Since we had all come down by road there was at our disposal a large number of chauffeurs and their cars, and it seemed a pity not to make use of them. We therefore offered the permanent service of these to the Southern Railway, pleased to be able to repay them in any way possible for the kindness they were showing us.[20]

In the end, the Dover docks ran quite smoothly and the undergraduates gloried in their victory at the end of the General Strike.

Such successes did not prevent the Government and its organs playing upon the public fear of disorder and chaos. On 8 May, the *British Gazette*, Churchill's incendiary to the dispute, reported that the transport and railway unions were going 'to do their utmost to paralyse and break down the supply of food and the necessaries of life' and 'That an organised attempt is being made to starve the people and to wreck the state . . .'. The *British Worker* responded, on 9 May, by dismissing the charge, claiming that 'The General Council has done nothing to imperil the food supplies; on the contrary, its members were instructed to co-operate with the Government in maintaining them.' There was, indeed, some truth in this counter claim for the trade unions helped to unload food ships at some ports. However, such help often led to claim and counter-claim by the Government and the trade unionists about their respective control of the situation regarding the movement of food and essential goods. As Tony Mason has indicated, such conflict of opinion abounded in the North East where the strike leaders claimed that Kingsley Wood, the Civil Commissioner, had called for dual control of the ports, thus indicating that the Government could not manage the movement of food without the support of the strikers. This was denied by Wood and the Government, and Mason cannot estimate whether the Government's Emergency Regulations collapsed or not. Nevertheless, a Home Office report to the Cabinet did indicate that picketing in the North East was effective: 'Police can protect the unloading of ships, but the difficulty is to get the convoys through the district just outside the city boundary.'[21]

Notwithstanding questions about the effectiveness of the strike, the measures of the Government were normally more than adequate to maintain the movement of food supplies. But how effective was the Government in maintaining law and order? There seems to some dispute here about the exact nature and zeal of Government action. On the one hand, Symons and Farman, accepting the TUC line, argue that the authorities became more aggressive and determined in their enforcement of law and order as the strike proceeded. On the other hand, Phillips argues that the Government took the necessary measures early and saw no need to become bullish about law and order.[22] The evidence tends to support the latter view. The Government aimed to augment the number of special constables in London to 50,000 on 5 May and set up a Civil Constabulary Reserve, drawn mainly from the Territorial Army and former soldiers. In addition, about 200,000 'second' reserve policemen were mobilised in England and Wales, outside London. But many of these forces were never used and, for instance, the Civil Constabulary Reserve, which had risen to 9,000 by the end of the strike, remained inactive throughout the dispute. As a result the Government had little need to use the military and naval forces which it had deployed throughout the country on the eve of the dispute. Indeed, there was little violence on 8 May when the 1,000 volunteers were escorted from London docks to Hyde Park by over a hundred lorries and twenty armoured cars, plus soldiers from the Welsh Guards and the Coldstream Guards. Given the fact that the Government never needed to use more than a small proportion of its volunteers and military resources, it is inconceivable that Baldwin, and the Government, ever took seriously their own claims that the General Strike was a revolutionary challenge to the constitution and, indeed, a civil war. As already suggested it is no surprise, then, that the Cabinet, which had felt the need to respond to the 'tremendous centralizing' of the trade unions by enforcing fuller consultation with the rank and file through a new Trades Disputes Bill, dropped the measure in anticipation of the end of the strike.[23] Only Winston Churchill's *British Gazette*, a disingenuous newspaper acting as a propaganda organ for the Government, seems to have seriously proclaimed an alternative viewpoint.

The simple fact is that the Government was in almost total control of the industrial situation, did not need to use all the emergency measures at its command and grew increasingly confident as the General Strike progressed. It felt that it was only a matter of time before the TUC would beat a course to its door. Within this context, the industrial conflict at local level was almost irrelevant, except, of course, that it was the rank and file's 'wonderful response' to the strike call which impinged itself on the minds of many trade union leaders.

The General Strike at local level: organisation and administration

It is an almost impossible task to assess the extent to which the strike was effective at the local level. For one thing, there are too few detailed studies in print and, for another, the surviving records convey a confused and transient picture of events. Nevertheless, given the complexity of the TUC's last minute arrangements – working through the existing trade union structures, setting up joint transport committees and giving local organisation responsibilities to the trades councils – the strike organisation was clearly impressive. Yet contemporary opinion tends to be more critical of the state of local organisation and administration than does more recent writing.

Despite the orders and intentions of the TUC, it was the trades councils, sometimes acting under the title of councils of action or strike committees, which ran the General Strike at local level. It is estimated that there were upwards of 500 of these, or similar, bodies active during the strike and Emile Burns obtained 190 replies in all, although only 131 offered detailed returns, to his Labour Research Department survey of their activities in 1926.[24] Of the 131 full returns, fifty-four came from Councils of Action, forty-five from Strike Committees, fifteen from Trades Councils, eight from Emergency Committees and nine from organisations given other descriptions, such as 'Vigilance Committee' at Lincoln and 'Disputes Advisory Council' at Aldershot.[25] Burns's feeling was that given that the trades councils and councils of action were 'suddenly asked to take a new and urgent task, without any but the vaguest suggestion of how they should carry it out' that 'viewed as a whole it was carried out effectively'.[26] Yet the fact is that they had assumed their responsibilities, of acting as local general councils, when the General Council had stipulated that the important functions, such as the issue of permits, should be organised by the local transport committees.

This view is strongly supported by Alan Clinton. However, he feels that the trades councils had anticipated their likely role before May 1926, for:

In September (1925) the President of the Birmingham Trades Council urged delegates to be fully prepared for the coming struggle, and early in 1926 the Bradford leaders said 'they strongly urge Trade Unionists to make preparations for the fight.'[27]

In addition he notes that at a 'Special Conference of Action' on 21 March 1926, fifty-two trades councils advertised their willingness to take action, stimulated partly by left-wing and communist activists. Local trades councils were also prepared for action in Huddersfield, Preston, Liverpool and many other centres. As a result, argues Clinton, almost every major urban centre had a well thought out strike organisation in place by the beginning of the dispute. Indeed, they acted so effectively that Jimmy Thomas began to fear that they would take over control of the strike, and they did form an effective rival organisation to the local authorities. As Clinton argues, 'After the General Strike many trades councils felt that they had done something to prove themselves.'[28]

Indeed, the trades councils and councils of action often operated around the clock, were composed of representatives of all the unions of the district, formed numerous sub-committees, issued permits, distributed relief, organised pickets, published bulletins, arranged transport, fixed up speakers for open-air meetings, and carried out a whole host of activities. Yet they varied immensely in the precise nature of the work they undertook. In the Labour Research Department survey of the 140 replies it would appear that about half, between seventy to seventy-twio, issued local strike bulletins, the titles including the Preston *Strike News*, *Brighton Bulletin*, *Westminster Worker*, the Newcastle *Workers' Chronicle* and *The Northern Light*, the bulletin of the Blaydon and Chopwell District Council of Action.[29] Of course, this exceeded the intentions of the TUC which felt that no local comment should be made and which ordered the cessation of all strike bulletins on 10 May.[30]

As already indicated, some Councils cultivated relations with co-operative societies whilst others did no such thing. In Bolton the co-operative society was 'largely a Conservative body and non-sympathetic' whilst the Coventry Co-operative Society seems to have been one of the most active during the strike – but even then the Council of Action had no definite arrangement with the society. The Co-operative Society, however, 'placed a car at the disposal of the Council of Action'.[31] The Bolton Council of Action was, in fact, very well provided for as far as transport was concerned, having fifty-seven motor bikes as well as cars and ordinary cycles.[32] Many Councils of Action/Trades Councils established close links with other similar bodies:

> Bolton developed lines of communication practically throughout Lancashire. Middlesbrough was in communication with a number of important centres; Wolverhampton established communications with Sheffield, Manchester, Shrewsbury. . .[33]

The vast array of Council of Action activities, of course, does not indicate the effectiveness of these forms of action and in some respects, as in the case of the issue of permits, confusion and a lack of local control certainly did impair the General Council's effort to control the distribution of food throughout Britain.

Burns also condemned the failure of the TUC and the trade unions to organise into the ten districts, apart from London, in England and Wales and the five in Scotland which the Government used as a basis of its administrative structure. Instead, there were, in England and Wales, at least 465 Trade Councils/Councils of Action active in the struggle – forty-eight in Yorkshire, (Area Three) fifty-two in London (Area Ten), and sixty-five in Lancashire (Area Two). The result is that the General Council had to communicate with at least 465 bodies in England and Wales, as well as to work with local transport committees, instead of being able to operate eleven district organisations.[34] There were some attempts at co-ordination: a meeting was organised to create a body responsible for London on 29 April 1926 but it never met during the General Strike.

Nevertheless, there were some successful examples of joint action. On Merseyside a single Council of Action was established to cover the towns of Birkenhead, Bootle and Wallasay and Liverpool. There were county federations of Councils of Action in Lanarkshire and east Glamorgan, and a shadowy body known as the North West Area Strike Council based on Manchester. More overt and effective were the Teeside Federation and the Northumberland and Durham General Council Joint Committee both of which acted with some success against the Government's strike-breaking machinery.[35] The latter was based on Newcastle and had little or no influence north of Ashington or south of Gateshead. Indeed, R. Page Arnot, active in organising the Newcastle Strike Committee doubted whether its bulletins reached as far north as Berwick, nor many places in south Durham.[36] Lily Davison, writing a few months after the General Strike, reflected that:

> Not until my services were transferred to the Northumberland and Durham General Council did I grasp the significance of this body, which had gradually grown up to direct the General Strike in the area. It had seemed to me that each union had run its own course in such matters as strike pay, keeping up the spirit of the members, issuing their own bulletins etc., and only on general questions such as permits etc. did the officials come together. This accounted for the mysterious meetings which certain officials attended, morning, noon and night, and in some cases left their members grumbling. It was on this Council that the local trade union

officials, members of other working organisations came down to earth . . . From the Council circular instructions were sent out by the newly formed Councils of Action, strike committees etc. To this Council, these bodies sent in reports, enquiries, etc. Step by step, this body learned its job and perfected its machinery.[37]

There were clearly many administrative failings as well as successes in the local attempts to make the General Strike effective. Burns, Mason, and other writers note the way in which most local organisations were not formed until 1 or 2 May, the many that did not have strike bulletins and the chaos surrounding their assumption of responsibility. Burns also points to the fragmented and sectional nature of Trades Council/Council of Action activities in Sheffield, Middlesbrough, St Albans and many other centres. Much weight has been given to these criticisms by some of the general and local surveys produced – although recent work tends, on the whole, to be rather more favourable to them than contemporary opinion allowed – pointing to the way in which the trades councils embodied the potent creative myth of trade union power.

This revised strand is evident in the case of Leeds, which came in for some strong criticism in 1927. At that time Raymond Postgate wrote that:

Where the strike committee had no sufficient authority there was always a danger that the private interests of various unions would cross those of the general solidarity of the workers, or as in Bradford, the (centre) of some of the textile union headquarters. Here the central officials, especially the Dyers, seemed to be chiefly occupied with securing the transport that they needed. The sister town of Leeds was even worse. It possessed no less than four rival Strike Committees, mutually jealous, and must have been the worse conducted town in England. The trouble was in part due to the possession by certain full-time officials of a direct telephone line to London. They clustered around this and remained isolated and superior. There were other personal difficulties which could, of course, have been resolved in twenty-four hours by a sufficiently decisive-minded plenipotentiary from London armed with proper authorisation.[38]

More recently, Tom Woodhouse has suggested that this picture is erroneous. In the first instance there were only three bodies – the Trades Council/Council of Action/Central Strike Committee, the local transport committee and the Leeds and District Joint Trade Union Committee (organised mainly by the General and Municipal Workers' Union). The first one derived its responsibilities from the General Council on 1 May, the second from the decision that local transport committees should review permits, and the third one from the fact that some unions objected to the militancy of the Leeds Trades Council and its informal associations with the National Minority Movement (the Communist trade union organisation) and, additionally, felt that trades councils should not interfere with the affairs of individual trade unions. In other words, there were good reasons for the divisions. Woodhouse also suggests that the strike organisation improved as the strike continued. There were about 36,000 to 40,000 Leeds workers directly involved in the dispute and 'Co-ordinated union organisation was improving immediately before the 12 May. . .'.[39]

Mass picketing appears to have been most effective in inducing such support. It was organised in towns such as Bolton, Leyton, Pontypridd, Stockton and Wakefield. At Bolton 2,280 pickets were mobilised in two days and thus permitted round the clock picketing with each picket on a four-hour duty and twenty hours off.[40]

This more favourable picture of the relative effectiveness of local strike organisations is supported by the evidence of Nottingham, where on 6 May it was announced that 'Mr. Harding the area food controller, has undertaken to move no food except by permission of the Strike Committee. He does not recognise the OMS.'[41] In Birmingham the strike was immediately effective, in bringing out workers and it was reported that 'The extent of the stoppage is much greater than anybody anticipated and all road, passenger, and carrying traffic has been stopped.'[42] In Gloucester, the port was brought to a halt and the local strike activity was marked whilst a similar picture of significant success emerges for Merseyside, the North East and in York.[43]

The General Strike in Bradford

Bradford, as a textile centre, was by no means a significant or sensitive area during the General Strike but, nevertheless, demonstrates how effective the strike organisation could be. The local trade union leaders responded magnificently to the strike call, partly in response to the fact that the miners had given them much moral and financial help during the textile dispute of 1925.

The Trades Council had anticipated the coming conflict but did not form the Council of Action until 3 May when, by resolution, it was decided to set up a body with the President and the Secretary of the Trades Council on it, secretary Walter Barber acting as the secretary of the Council of Action. On 4 May it set up a sub-committee to deal with the issue of permits and a full emergency committee to deal with general problems. The Council was also divided into six trade groups, *A* for transport, *B* for building, *C* for engineering, *D* for textiles, *E* for printing and *F* for miscellaneous. It thus, effectively, incorporated the local transport committee, groups A, within its organisation. Each group had a convenor and sent two representatives to the Central Executive Committee which was also composed of the President, Secretary and one other member of the Bradford Trades Council.[44]

The Bradford Council of Action was well organised and attempted to act in a model manner. Indeed, on 5 May it refrained from issuing permits after discussions with various transport unions and before the TUC communicated with it for the first time on 7 May. Indeed, Barber noted that:

> so far as Bradford is concerned the call was largely responded to. Some little difficulty, however, did arise in the Transport section in consequence of misrepresentation of the TUC's instructions and the unorganised state of the Road Transport section. We were, however, able to cripple . . . Transport.
>
> Not a single train was run after the evening of May 3rd until the afternoon of Tuesday May 11th when a very small skeleton service was attempted. The Executive immediately considered the position and gave instructions through the Engineering Group for the withdrawal of all power house men at Valley Road.[45]

The engineers at Valley Road generated the electricity which ran the trams.

The Council of Action also ensured that local communications were good and produced three copies of *The Bradford Worker*, which sold 10,000, 6,500 and 10,000 copies.[46] It also prided itself that there was little violence and few arrests, although in nearby Shipley eight Communists were arrested under the Emergency Powers Act, 1920, 'for being in possession of documents likely to cause mutiny or unrest among the people, police, soldiers and firemen'.[47]

The mood of the Bradford workers was fairly pro-strike. Indeed, this was well illustrated at a mass meeting of about 10,000 people on Sunday, 9 May when most of the local prominents from the Labour Party and the trade unions spoke. W. Hirst, MP, J. H. Palin, MP, Walter Barber, Alderman A. Pickles and many others were present, and Barber caught the mood of the meeting when he stated that 'The workers were not to blame for the dispute, it was the Government and the ruling class.'[48] The class dimension of the dispute was strongly emphasised.

The relationship between the trade union movement, the local ILP and the Labour Party, were of the closest, especially since Barber also acted as the secretary of the Bradford Labour Party until 1927 when the Trades Disputes Act made that situation difficult. This closeness was particularly evident in the City Council where, on 12 May, the Labour councillors attacked the chairman of the Transport Committee, Councillor Irvine Smith (Liberal) for attempting to organise a skeleton tramway service without the approval of the transport committee. In addition, Councillor R. Ruth asked the pertinent question, 'Has the chairman found whether the operation of the Emergency Act is tantamount to the breaking of all agreements between employers and employees?[49] If that was the case then the charge that the workers had broken their contracts by striking would have been hard to sustain.

In the final analysis, the General Strike was called off and an organised retreat had to be arranged. The evidence suggests that this was achieved with remarkable felicity in Bradford. Walter Barber was pleased to report 'that every tramwayman has been re-instated' with no reductions.[50] Most workers appear to have returned with little difficulty. The problems on the railways were quickly settled, the Bradford Dyers agreed to pay £100 and the cost of a court case designed to establish the rule of law in acquiescence to the Bradford Dyers' Association which, under existing agreements, could have claimed £1 compensation for every one of the 6,000 to 7,000 dyers who had broken their contracts by coming out on strike.

In summary then, support for the General Strike in Bradford was almost one hundred per cent, there was little violence, the

Council of Action was well organised and generally carried out the bidding of the TUC, when it was informed of its instructions, the Labour Party gave its full support and the return to work was relatively amicable and involved little rancour. If support in Bradford was almost total, however, how much support was there for the conflict elsewhere?

Rank and file response

Much of the effectiveness of the General Strike can be measured in the numbers of workers who responded to the strike call when they were asked to do so. By and large, local studies suggest that the majority of those who were asked to leave work did so. There may have been up to 40,000 workers directly participating in the dispute in Leeds, and about 7,000 workers in York – 6,000 of them railwaymen, 4,422 of them being members of the NUR.[51] In Merseyside up to 100,000 workers may have come out, including 70,000 or so in Liverpool and 6,000 building trade workers.[52] Such a high level of support seems typical in both industrial and rural, as well as mining, areas. J. H. Porter, writing about the General Strike in the rural county of Devon has challenged the assumption that the General Strike had a negligible impact upon rural areas: 'The evidence suggests that within the limits of its industrial structure Devon trade unionists responded to the unions' decisions to support the miners, and did so in a particularly hostile climate of opinion and in a county which was difficult to organise.'[53] The fact is that in the major towns of Portsmouth, Plymouth, Torquay, Newton Abbot and Exeter – there was significant support and, even though the building workers and the printers were somewhat fitful in their response, railwaymen and municipal tramway drivers were resolute in their support of the strike. On average more than 80 per cent of the railway workers of the Great Western Railway, more or less everybody except the clerical and supervisory staff, were out on strike for the nine days and beyond.[54] In the case of the Plymouth tramway men the attempt of a small number of blacklegs to operate the service led to the Plymouth tram riot on 8 May, which cut across the peaceful image presented by the famous football match, of the same day, in which the strikers beat the police 2–1. Nevertheless, the tram workers drifted back quickly thereafter and 85 per cent were back at work by the 12 May.[55]

The Plebs League conducted an independent survey of the response to the General Strike which was published in *A Worker's History of the Great Strike* by Postgate, Wilkinson and Horrabin. It recognised that the railwaymen in the NUR and ASLEF were the 'rock-like centre to the strike' and attempted to assess the strengths and weaknesses of the various towns, classifying them as Class I, a 90 to 100 per cent response, Class II, where the response was impressive but where there was some weakening or a lack of information, and Class III where there was weakness in one section or another. In all areas of Britain Section I included at least two-thirds of the areas and towns listed, and there were very few towns and areas in Section III. There was undoubtedly some exaggeration here, the Plebs League reporters were, perhaps, too dazzled by the enthusiasm of the strikers. Nevertheless, this impressionistic survey suggests that there was widespread support for the strike and that in the vast majority of cases most of the first line workers came out.[56]

A full and accurate picture of the rank and file support for the strike is not possible given the absence of surveys of hundreds of the localities and regions which it affected. Nevertheless, certain points have emerged. In the first place there seems to have been a 'magnificent' rank and file response in all localities, even if the local strike organisation was often imperfect. Secondly, it would appear that wherever there were significant numbers of trade-union organised industrial and service workers in an area the vast majority came out when requested. Thirdly, the much maligned railwaymen – often accused with J. H. Thomas, their leader, of not wanting the strike, were the most resolute supporters of the General Strike and, subsequently, often the most vulnerable to victimisation. Indeed, at the end of the strike 98 per cent of the locomotive and firemen were still out. But strong support from the rank and file, even in the absence of a far from perfect strike organisation, was far from being a guarantee that the authorities would be unable to manage. Successful strike activity often went side by side with effective counter-measures by the authorities.

The effectiveness of the local authorities

It has already been suggested that the Government was confident in its ability to control the movement of foodstuffs and essential goods, so much so that its threatened legislation to control strikes was abandoned before the end of the General Strike. This reflected the growing confidence that its emergency measures were working at the regional and local levels. Indeed, in most localities, other than in some mining districts, the authorities retained overall control of foodstuffs and essential services. Indeed, many local surveys, whilst testifying to the large amount of support for the strike, indicate that the authorities were in control.

Most towns appointed officers and committees to keep food and coal supplies flowing and, for instance, Plymouth appointed a Food Officer, a Coal Officer and an 'Emergency Committee', composed of the Mayor and two councillors. They called for volunteers, and by 11 May there were about 24,000 volunteers in the South-West District compared with 25,000 in the North-East of England.[57] In Liverpool, which handled about one-fifth of Britain's total imports the authority had the right to introduce coal rationing and commandeer vehicles, and had enrolled over 1,200 special constables by 8 May. Two battleships and three destroyers entered the Mersey, the former landing food supplies, and a troopship arrived from Plymouth with two fully equipped battalions. In addition, there were more than 20,000 volunteers, mainly white-collar workers and students. In other words the authorities carried enough weight to ensure that absolutely vital supplies kept moving.[58] In Birmingham, the Council worked through its existing sub-committees and with an Emergency Sub-Committee to maintain gas, electricity, water, refuse collection and transport and was supported by a number of voluntary bodies including the OMS, which had 1,105 volunteers by 3 May and 11,876 by the end of the strike – although only 1,990 were used.[59] In York, the authorities were similarly geared up to deal with the dispute and although the precise numbers given by the Volunteer Service Committee seem to fluctuate 'it is clear that the fears of the Conservatives were much exaggerated because, once the strike started, more volunteers came forward than could be used – and police were able to maintain order without assistance.'[60] Although there is some doubt about the effectiveness of the authorities, particularly from the evidence of the North-East and the accounts of what occurred in South Wales, the overwhelming impression is that they coped adequately with the dispute and did not need to use the large number of volunteers, and resources at their disposal. There was not the great breakdown of authority which was feared by the Government and local Conservative organisations.

Nevertheless, in one major respect the authorities, and private companies, could do little. The railways were effectively brought to a halt by the strike of NUR and ASLEF members. In the case of all the major railway companies, the LMSR, the LNER, the GWR and SR, there were greater efforts made to move passengers rather than freight. The welter of statistics available suggests that most companies were moving well under one per cent of their freight volume on 5 May, although this had risen to between 3.4 and 8.0 per cent for the different companies by the 12 May. Passenger volume varied between 3.7 per cent and 5.1 per cent on 5 May and had risen to between 13.4 and 22.4 per cent. Quite clearly the companies were able to run more trains as the strike wore on, using the managerial staff and volunteers, but around ninety-eight per cent of the NUR and ASLEF members stayed out, with only a small number trickling back before the end of the dispute, although all of the big four railway companies were able to improve their normal passenger service from less than four per cent at the beginning of the strike to between twelve and nineteen per cent by the end.[61]

There were also higher risks to life and limb when volunteer train drivers tried to maintain a service, and many minor accidents occurred. One such accident on the Huddersfield to Manchester line was not untypical: 'Six trains passed through Huddersfield on Saturday. The 8.30am train to Manchester collided with the level crossing gate at Clayton Bridge. Only slight damage was done. The train was able to proceed.'[62]

Notwithstanding the failures in rail transport, the local authorities and regional administration managed to keep control of the basic structure of administration without having to call upon all their available resources. Indeed, there were some marginal improvements in rail transport as the General Strike continued.

Policing and violence

The vast majority of strike committees and councils of action abided by the instruction of the General Council, constantly reiterated in the *British Worker*, that they must avoid conflict and preserve law and order. This edict was accepted even when the General Council sought to reduce the number of permits and when mass picketing became a reality. Consequently, serious violence was rare. Nevertheless, there were the tram riots in Plymouth, some disturbances in London where there was harassment on the South Side as a result of attempts to unload food cargoes, some violence in the coalfields, and large unorganised crowds rioted in Hull and Middlesbrough.[63] Where there was the likelihood of conflict with the police 'Workers' Defence Corps' were organised, as in Leeds, in Methil, Fife, and about a dozen other areas.[64] In fact, very little violence occurred in these areas – although the Communist-inspired march from Castleford to Leeds did lead to violence along York Road in Leeds. But there were some centres which faced significant conflict.

The worst violence occurred in Glasgow, where around 200 arrests were made as a result of clashes between the police and the miners. There were also serious clashes on Tyneside and Doncaster. Indeed, according to the Home Secretary there were 1,760 arrests made under the emergency regulations during the General Strike, 1,389 for acts of violence and disorder and 150 for incitement by speech or writing. Of these, 583 were charges brought by county police forces of which 396 were in Northumberland, Durham and the West Riding of Yorkshire. In addition, there were more than 5,000 arrests made under the ordinary regulations.[65] The record of prosecutions provided by the Transport and General Workers' Union indicates that of 174 charges against their members, seventy-nine were in London, thirty-six in Glasgow, twenty-four in Birmingham and fourteen in Leeds.[66]

It is estimated that 2,500 Communists, half the CPGB membership, were amongst those arrested. In the West Riding of Yorkshire, action was taken against the Communist 'strongholds' in Castleford and Shipley. On 9 May it was reported that:

At Pontefract yesterday Isobel Brown, who said that her last permanent address was Moscow, was committed for three months in the second division for having delivered a speech at Castleford on Wednesday likely to cause disaffection. She admitted she had come from London to gain recruits for the Communist Party but denied any attempt to stir up strife.[67]

She had been arrested in the Bradford district where there 'was a very small Communist Party somewhere in the background, whose roots seemed to be in Shipley because some of the most important members lived there'.[68] The context of this incident is further elaborated by Margaret Morris who wrote that:

> Vic Feather [a later General Secretary of the TUC] only narrowly escaped being arrested while helping to produce the *Bradford Strike Bulletin*. Nothing had been published to justify arresting those producing the paper but one of the helpers, a Communist called Isobel Brown, had made a speech at a public meeting urging the troops not to act as strike-breakers. Vic Feather had just arrived at the Shipley I.L.P. rooms with a load of duplicating paper when there was a loud knocking at the door. Acting on instinct he vanished to the toilets. Everything went quiet. After about twenty minutes he emerged and found no one there. Later he discovered that Isobel and her husband and sixteen others had been arrested; she was accused of inciting troops to disaffection and was sentenced to three months in prison for her speech.[69]

Yet, given the size of the General Strike, the fact that it involved one and three quarter million workers supporting one million miners and engendered much class conflict, the level of violence and the number of arrests was small. No one was killed as a result of violence, although there were some near misses. Indeed, there could have been significant loss of life when the Edinburgh to Kings Cross express train was derailed at the North East pit village of Cromlington, which eventually led to the imprisonment of eight men. Yet the fact is that there were hundreds if not thousands of minor incidents which provoked jostling, the beating up of 'blacklegs' and the like, but little that threatened life. As a result, as already indicated, the vast majority of the Civil Constabulary and the 'second' reserve policeman were not used. And Hastings, writing on Birmingham, states that:

> Although Julian Symons lists Birmingham among the cities where 'there were more or less serious riots' outbreaks of violence were rare and much less serious than incidents during the 1911 Rail

Strike, when pitched battles were fought between police and strikers. . . . As in the North-East most of the trouble that erupted was closely inter-related with transport and picketing. On 5 May for example, strong contingents of Staffordshire and Birmingham Police with reinforcements of special constabulary, released seven Midland Red buses from Bearwood Garage, in an attempt to run a skeleton service between Quinton and Birmingham. They were immobilised, however, by strikers in Broad Street who deflated their tyres.[70]

Similar events were repeated many times during the nine-day dispute. But the fact is that the trades councils and the strike organisations were determined to maintain discipline and to temper any tendency towards lawless behaviour. The General Strike was perceived by the majority of trade unionists to be an industrial dispute without political connotations or threats to the British Constitution, no matter what the Government believed. This view was not always shared by some of the Communist activists.

Communist influence

The Communist Party of Great Britain had been formed in London in 1920, and was reformed at Leeds in 1921. Throughout the early 1920s the Government had been extremely worried and suspicious about its revolutionary activities, and was particularly so after it formed the National Minority Movement and encouraged the development of the power of this body within the trade union movement. As a result, on 13 October 1925 the Cabinet decided to prosecute the leading members of the Party for sedition and arrested twelve of them on 14 October. They were charged with unlawfully conspiring to publish seditious libels and to incite others to common breaches of the Incitement to Mutiny Act of 1797. Found guilty, they were imprisoned for periods of six months or a year, which meant that some, such as Robin Page Arnot, were released just before the General Strike. Not surprisingly, the authorities bore down on the Communists during the dispute, thus exaggerating the real importance of Communist influence. The fact is that there were many Communists helping the strike effort throughout the country but little evidence that they dominated the councils of action or strike committees. There were five Communists on the Central Strike Committee in Glasgow, two on the Town Strike Committee at Falkirk, four on the Middlesbrough Central Strike Committee, three on the Barrow Council of Action, and there were many other strike bodies where one or two Communists were present. But it was only at Battersea, in London, that the Communist Party carried any significant influence, with ten Communist Party members on the committee of 124, of whom four were on the seven-member executive committee.[71] Communists do not appear to have caused much dissension within the strike organisations, although there was an attempt by the Communist-inspired NUWM (National Unemployed Workers' Movement) to join the Liverpool Council of Action. Communist support was accepted because it was aimed at supporting the strike effort, not because of its revolutionary potential. As James Klugmann, a prominent lifelong Communist, has written:

> The Party well knew that on the eve of the strike the workers were eager for action, but not in any sense in a revolutionary mood. They were ready to fight on economic issues, to show their solidarity with the miners to defy the threats of government – but they were *not* ready to challenge the social system. The Party knew, too, that many of those taking part in this great unprecedented strike, particularly those most deeply involved in it, could in a few days develop further politically than in the years of more 'normal' times. Its problem was how to help to organise the struggle, develop the local leaderships of the Councils of Action, lift the level of the strike, put forward step by step, new lines of action, and prepare, as far as possible, for continued struggle when, as it had so often warned, the General Council capitulated. Not easy![72]

In the final analysis the Communist Party helped the strikers, published thousands of copies of the *Workers' Weekly* and the *Workers' Bulletin*, circulated manifestoes and gave a tremendous amount of support for the dispute but not in its wildest dreams did it imagine that it would dominate or greatly influence the course of events. Indeed, Government victimisation of the communists greatly exaggerated their true importance.

Conclusion

The General Strike, by its very diversity and local and regional variation, presents historians with the complex problem of how to assess what occurred. The Tory press raged against the revolutionary threats which it posed to Britain, and the Government was wont to play upon such fears. Notwithstanding these carefully nurtured concerns, it is obvious that there was no revolutionary threat, that the level of violence and conflict was minimal, and that the TUC's strike organisation was remarkably successful at the national and local level at a time when the Government and the regional and local authorities felt that they had kept matters well under control. There may appear to be a contradiction in suggesting that both the strikers and the authorities performed their duties well in the dispute but this is not so in the sense that both generally accepted the spheres of control – picketing was to be lawful and the troops were not to be brought in unless matters got out of hand. If there was little conflict it was because neither the strikers nor the authorities wanted it, just as much as the fact that as long as the authorities had overall control of food and essential services they could allow the almost complete shutdown of the railways. For nine days Britain experienced a significant shutdown of its normal life without the Government losing control of the situation. Indeed, as the General Strike continued it is clear that the Government became more confident of its position just as much as the TUC began to fear for the whole trade union movement. In the end, of course, it did not matter that the strikers responded magnificently to the strike call, or that support was still almost a hundred per cent on 12 May, for the dispute was to be settled by a coterie of national trade union leaders and not by the rank and file who had given their fervent support to the miners.

Notes

1 Bevin speech in the TUC General Council, *Special Conference of Executives*, 20 January 1927.

2 Cook, *Nine Days*, p. 16.

3 Burns, *General Strike*.

4 R. P. Arnot, 'The General Strike in the North-East', in L. M. Munby, ed., *The Luddites and Other Essays* (1971); Baines and Bean, 'Merseyside'; Hastings, 'Birmingham 1926'; Hills, *York*; Mason, *North East*; Porter, 'Devon'; J. Whyman, 'The General Strike: its Impact on the Medway Towns', *Cantium*, 3, 1971; Wyncoll, 'Nottingham'; Williams,

'Gloucestershire'; Woodhouse, 'Leeds'. Also R. Mace, 'Battersea, London'; S. Bhaumik, 'Glasgow'; E. W. Edwards, 'The Pontypridd Area' and S. Benton, 'Sheffield' in Morris, *General Strike*; P. Carter, 'The West of Scotland'; I. MacDougal, 'Edinburgh'; E. and R. Frow, 'Manchester Diary'; P. Wyncoll, 'The East Midlands'; G. Barnsby, 'The Black Country'; R. P. Hastings, 'Birmingham'; H. Francis, 'South Wales'; J. Attfield and J. Lee, 'Deptford and Lewisham' and A. Tuckett, 'Swindon' in Skelley, *General Strike*.

5   Phillips, *General Strike*, p. 140.

6   Crook, *General Strike*, p. 413.

7   K. Laybourn, *British Trade Unionism c 1770–1990*, Sutton, Stroud, 1990, p. 142.

8   *Workers' Chronicle*, 8 May 1926.

9   Interview with Mr Skinner, a retired power worker, conducted in 1979. In the possession of Professor Keith Laybourn.

10   Baines and Bean, 'Merseyside', pp. 251–2.

11   H. Duckworth, 'Dover Dockers. A Diary kept by one of them, with Appreciation', now deposited in the London School of Economics Library, Coll. 0760. Look at Document Section.

12   On 11 May 500,000 copies were produced in London, 40,000 in Cardiff, 30,000 in Glasgow and 70,000 in Manchester.

13   Burns, *Councils in Action*, chapter 5. Of 140 trades councils' councils of action seventy-three had some type of arrangements with the local co-operative societies and sixty-seven had none. Five co-operatives gave money and twenty-nine established some type of credit arrangements.

14   Cab 29/260 ST (24) 23rd meeting, 14. Cab 27/331 S.T. Bull, 10 May.

15   Cab 23/331, S. T. Bull, 10 May.

16   Duckworth, 'Dover Dockers'.

17   *Ibid.*, p. 4.

18   *Ibid.*, p. 8.

19   *Ibid.*

20   *Ibid*, referring to 7 May 1926.

21   Mason, *North East*, pp.54–88, quoting PRO, Cab 27/331, Home Office Situation, No. 6, 7 May 1926 and *An Account of the Proceedings of the Northumberland and Durham General Council and Joint Stock Committee*.

22   Symons, *General Strike*, pp. 194–5; Farman, *General Strike,*, pp. 197–9; Phillips, *General Strike*, pp. 160–5.

23   Jones, *Whitehall Diary*, **II**, pp. 13, 15, 36.

24   Burns, *Councils in Action* and look at Document Section.

25   *Ibid.*, p. 13.

26   *Ibid.*, chapter IV.

27   A. Clinton, 'Trades Councils from the beginning of the Twentieth Century to the Second World War', unpublished PhD, University of

London, 1973, p. 214, quoting *Town Crier*, 11 September 1925 and Bradford Trades and Labour Council, *Yearbook, 1926*, p. 3.

28 *Ibid.*, p. 234.
29 Burns, *Councils in Action*, chapter IV.
30 *General Council Bulletin*, 4 May 1926.
31 Burns, *Councils in Action*, p. 58.
32 *Ibid.*, p. 62.
33 *Ibid.*, p. 64.
34 *Ibid.*, p. 76.
35 *Ibid.*, p. 80; Mason, *North East*, pp. 22–5.
36 Mason, *North East*, quoting an interview with R. P. Arnot, 19 November 1963.
37 Plebs, August 1926, pp. 279–81, quoted in Mason, *General Strike*, p. 24.
38 Postgate, Wilkinson and Horrabin, *Workers' History*, pp. 46–7. The same quote is given incorrectly in Woodhouse, 'Leeds' p. 252.
39 Woodhouse, 'Leeds', pp. 257, 261.
40 A. Scheps, 'Trade Unions and Government 1925–7', unpublished D. Phil., Oxford University, 1972, p. 346.
41 Wyncoll, 'Nottingham', p. 176.
42 Hastings, 'Birmingham', p. 256.
43 Williams, 'Gloucestershire'; Baines and Bean, 'Merseyside'; Arnot, 'North East'; Hills, *York*.
44 Letter from W. Barber to W. Citrine, 21 May 1926, deposited in West Yorkshire District Archives, Bradford, items 57 and 57/1, 56D80/10/2.
45 *Ibid.*
46 *The Bradford Worker*, 8, 11 and 13 May 1926, W.Y.D.A., Bradford, 56 D8/10/4.
47 *The Bradford Worker*, 8 May 1926.
48 *Ibid.*, 11 May 1926.
49 *Ibid.*, 13 May 1926.
50 Look at note 46.
51 Hills, *York*, p. 14.
52 Baines and Bean, 'Merseyside', pp. 248–51.
53 Porter, 'Devon', p. 355.
54 *Ibid.*, p. 337.
55 *Ibid.*, pp. 341–3.
56 Postgate, Wilkinson and Horrabin, *Workers' History*, pp. 28–32.
57 Porter, 'Devon', pp. 335–6.
58 Baines and Bean,'Merseyside', p. 254.
59 Hastings, 'Birmingham', pp. 253–5.
60 Hills, *York*, p. 12.
61 Crook, *General Strike*, p. 390; Phillips, *General Strike*, pp. 163, 210.

62 *Yorkshire Observer*, 9 May 1926.

63 Cab 27/260, ST 24/25, 9 May 1926.

64 Burns, *Councils in Action.*, p. 143.

65 Quoted in Phillips, *General Strike*, p. 203.

66 T&GWU GEC, Sub-committee report on the General Strike, quoted in Phillips, *General Strike*, p. 204.

67 *Yorkshire Observer*, 9 May 1992.

68 D. A. Wilson, 'From Bradford', in Skelley, *General Strike*, p. 353.

69 Morris, *General Strike*, p. 86.

70 Hastings, 'Birmingham', pp. 263–4.

71 *Workers' Weekly*, 21 May 1926 provides a full listing of the participation of Communist Party members on Councils of Action and Strike Committees.

72 J. Klugmann, 'Marxism, Reformism and the General Strike', in Skelley, *General Strike*, p. 79.

4

The Settlement

A. J. Cook wrote of the General Strike that 'The workers acted as one. Splendid discipline! Splendid loyalty!' He then asked the vital question, 'Why was the strike called off?'[1] It is a question which has occupied the minds of both historians and contemporaries alike. Cook's own conclusion was that the conspiratorial Jimmy Thomas and other right-wing leaders of the TUC were opposed to it from the start and that they were seeking to end the dispute with indecent haste.[2] The Communist Party of Great Britain held similar views, vilifying the General Council in its exaggerated statement that its:

> decision to call off the General Strike is the greatest crime that has ever been permitted, not only against the miners, but against the working class of Great Britain and the whole world.
> The Right Wing in the General Council bears direct responsibility for throwing away the workers' weapons and leaving them alone and defenceless.[3]

Although many alternative views have been expressed since 1926, there is a general acceptance that these contemporary assessments are close to the mark. Indeed, Farman, Renshaw and Phillips all point to the TUC's concern to call off the strike before it wound down of its own accord or before local leaders assumed the power of the centre of the trade union movement. Indeed, Jimmy Thomas's comments in the House of Commons that the strike had to be called off before 'it got out of hand', tends to confirm this impression.[4] Obviously, the precise contours of the argument alter from writer to writer but the message is broadly the same – the TUC General Council sought a pretext to call off the strike at the first opportunity. It therefore welcomed the intervention of Sir Herbert Samuel, chairman of the Coal Commission, who offered his services to settle the dispute. The TUC leaders deluded themselves into thinking that some arrangement with Samuel would be the basis of an honourable settlement when they must have known that any agreement would in effect be an act of surrender.

A constitutional strike

The TUC was always sensitive to the charge that the General Strike was a direct challenge to the British constitution and parliamentary authority. Such an accusation was mounted by Winston Churchill and the *British Gazette*. On 3 May, in the House of Commons, Churchill accused the General Council of challenging the British constitution[5], a view repeated in the *British Gazette*, 5 May, under the headline, 'Hold-up of the Nation':

> The general strike is in operation, expressing in no uncertain terms a direct challenge to ordered government . . . an effort to force upon some 42,000,000 British citizens the will of less than 4,000,000 others engaged in the vital services of the country.[6]

The Commons debate of 3 May is, indeed, an interesting indication of how the three major political parties viewed the General Strike. On the one hand, J. H. Thomas emphasised the Labour, and TUC, line which abhorred a General Strike which challenged the constitution whilst emphasising that the impending strike was not something that says 'We want to overthrow everything. It is merely a plain, economic, industrial dispute, where the workers say we want justice.'[7] At the other extreme, there was the attitude of the Conservative Party as expressed by Churchill. Between the two extremes lay David Lloyd George, the effective leader of the Liberal Party, who saw the General Strike as a mistake since it was designed to get the Government to take action and did not arise from an ordinary dispute. Yet, equally, he felt that it was 'a very serious mistake' for the Government to announce that it would not negotiate under duress.

Opinion was quite clearly divided, but there is no doubt that the Government won the debate. Not all Liberals blamed both sides, as Lloyd George had done. Indeed, Sir John Simon, one of the Liberal Party's leading lights, was particularly vitriolic in his condemnation of the strikers both in his writings and in the House of Commons, suggesting that their victory in changing the will of Parliament would have 'meant the overthrow of Constitutional government'.[8] And the Government published Simon's parliamentary speech in the *British Gazette* on 8 May. Baldwin made similar comments in his BBC radio broadcast on 8 May in which he claimed that he was 'a man of peace' but was unwilling 'to surrender the safety and security of the British constitution.'[9] Baldwin referred to the constitutional question again in a speech on the BBC on 10 May. The Government was further buoyed up by the Astbury Judgment of 11 May, which supported the National Sailor and Firemen's Union in its refusal to allow the TUC to order its members to leave work. Astbury argued that the General Strike was 'illegal and contrary to the law', since under the 1906 Act, 'no trade dispute had been alleged or shown to exist in any case of the unions affiliated, except the miners' case'.[10]

It seems doubtful whether the General Strike was illegal, for if it had been then there would have been no reason for the Government to have introduced the Trades Dispute Act in 1927. Nevertheless, the charges that it was unconstitutional, and thus illegal, remained to the fore, helped by the fact that the Government held control of the airwaves. John Reith, the Director General of the BBC, may have declared the BBC's independence during the dispute but this was little more than a facade, for Reith ensured that rival broadcasts, such as the one that the Archbishop of Canterbury had planned for 7 May, never occurred. Indeed, J. R. MacDonald and David Lloyd George were both blocked in their attempts to broadcast to the nation by the Cabinet on 11 May, although it was Reith who explained to these politicians that the BBC could not be seen to be approving something which was illegal.[11]

The General Council countered the accusation that it was acting unconstitutionally by stressing that the dispute was industrial and not political. The *British Worker* maintained, on 10 May, that:

It is merely . . . fantastic for the Prime Minister to pretend that the Trade Unions are engaged in an attack upon the Constitution of the Country. Every instruction issued by the General Council is evidence of their determination to maintain the struggle strictly on the basis of an industrial dispute. They have ordered every member taking part to be exemplary in his conduct and not to give any cause for police interference.[12]

In other words, the strike was presented in the most moderate of terms. In essence, however, the TUC was faced with a number of problems. On the one hand, it realised that it could not make the strike fully effective without inconveniencing the public and losing its support. Secondly, the TUC realised that it was directly challenging the Government in the sense that its only objective was to force it to intervene in order to prevent further wage reductions in the coal industry. This was secondary pressure on a grand scale, for which there was no precedent and to which it was clear that the Government would not, indeed could not, accede. There were constitutional implications in calling a general strike which the TUC would have liked to have avoided. The emergence of the Samuel initiative was thus seen as a lifeline to a much worried General Council.

The Samuel intervention

Even before Samuel's intervention, the General Council had already grasped at straws in seeking a settlement. The Archbishop of Canterbury's peace initiative on behalf of both Anglicans and Non-Conformists was welcomed, but got nowhere. The secret conversations between J. H. Thomas and two former Liberal ministers, Lord Wimborne and Lord Reading, faired little better although they may be seen as an attempt by Thomas to gain some support for his talks with Samuel. It was the Samuel talks which provided the best opportunity for a settlement.

Sir Herbert Samuel was at San Vigilio in the Italian Lakes at the beginning of the General Strike. On 3 May he telegraphed Baldwin to offer his services as a negotiator and, despite rejection, quickly returned to Britain to be of service in the dispute. On his return, on 6 May, he contacted various people, including Jimmy Thomas, and met the Negotiating Committee of the TUC at 3.00pm on 7 May at the home of Sir Abe Bailey, a South African millionaire friend of Jimmy Thomas. He also met the Mining Association representatives on the same day, although they rejected his suggestions that the existing national minimum wage be retained, that reductions could be made on basic wages at the district level and that a National Wages Board be established. The Negotiating Committee of the General Council was more disposed to these views, being particularly attracted by the idea of a National Wages Board and it was here that Samuel concentrated his efforts.

None the less, Samuel found his initiative thwarted by the Government. It had rejected his early overtures of help and on 7 May Government representatives informed Samuel, as he informed the TUC Negotiating Committee on 8 May, that 'ministers were not prepared to negotiate either privately or openly'.[13] The Negotiating Committee agreed to keep the Government rebuff from the miners and their colleagues on the General Council and continued to contemplate an arrangement whereby, if a settlement could be worked out in detail, wage reductions would be conceded if the Government provided a temporary subsidy.

Samuel continued his talks with the TUC and the first version of the 'Samuel Memorandum' was circulated to the General Council on the evening of 8 May, and shown to the miners the following day.[14] It was broadly based upon the Samuel Report, with demands for the reorganisation of the coal industry and wage reductions for one year, but included the added device of an impartial National Wages Board to maintain a watch over the reorganisation of the industry and the local wage agreements which might be agreed.

However, it was soon clear that the miners were as obdurate as the Government and would not accept the 'Samuel Memorandum', their sub-committee and full executive rejecting it on 9 May. They were suspicious about negotiations and unwilling to bend on the issue of wage reductions. As Cook wrote:

On Sunday, May 9th it was quite evident that these discussions and pow wows had reached a stage where the Negotiating Committee and the leaders of the Labour Party felt that something tangible had been secured to justify a move towards calling off the General Strike.[15]

The TUC Negotiating Committee therefore raised the possibility
of a new agreement in which wage reductions would only be
implemented after reorganisation had occurred. But the miners's
leaders would not contemplate anything which involved a wage
cut. As Citrine wrote of this meeting, on the evening of Monday,
10 May: 'Miner after miner got up and, speaking with an intensity
of feeling, affirmed that the miners could not go back to work on a
reduction in wages.' Arthur Pugh, putting the TUC attitude,
suggested that the miners were ' living in a fool's paradise' and
that they would be defeated by 'a process of attrition'.[16] Ultimately, after an adjournment, the miners accepted the
agreement if the TUC would include a statement to the effect that
they saw no reason for wage reductions since reorganisation
would make them unnecessary.[17] The TUC took no such action,
met Samuel on the morning of 11 May to suggest that the miners
were unmoveable, and met him again in the afternoon to form
what became the final version of the 'Samuel Memorandum'.
Then Samuel went away to secure the signatures of his former
colleagues on the Coal Commission, which he failed to achieve
because of their fundamental opposition to the renewal of a
subsidy.

In the meantime, the General Council met the miners on the
evening of 11 May, indicating that the memorandum was 'a fair
basis for negotiating a settlement'. Again, Cook reveals the extent
to which the miners felt suspicious of the whole process of
negotiation:

> We were told these proposals were unalterable, could not be
> amended, that we had to accept them *en bloc* as this was the
> unanimous decision of the T.U.C.
>
> Mr. Pugh was continually pressed and questioned by Mr.
> Herbert Smith, myself, and my colleagues about what the
> guarantees mentioned were, and who had given them. We got no
> answer. But J. H. Thomas said to me personally, when I asked him
> whether the Government would accept the Samuel proposals and
> who were his guarantors: 'You may not trust my word, but will
> you accept the word of a British Gentleman who has been
> Governor of Palestine.'[18]

After that meeting, with a two-hour recess the miners rejected
the memorandum, could not agree to wage reductions, and
objected to the General Council decision to end the stoppage.

Thereafter, the General Council asked Citrine to organise an interview with the Prime Minister for noon 12 May. According to Citrine a telephone call from Patrick Gower, one of the Prime Minister's secretaries indicated that Baldwin 'wants to know whether you have any news for him. He has been sitting up for you. Do you want to see him this evening?' After counselling the General Council, Citrine replied that:

> The General Council instruct me to say that they will be ready to see the Prime Minister tomorrow at twelve o'clock noon, positively. 'All right, Mr. Citrine, we may take that as fixed.' Our fate was decided in those few seconds. Our decision to see the Prime Minister meant plainly to them the calling off of the General Strike.[19]

The end of the General Strike had come.

The events which followed are almost legendary. The representatives of the General Council were met on the doorstep of 10 Downing Street at noon on 12 May by Sir Horace Wilson and were only allowed in once the calling off of the General Strike had been confirmed. In their subsequent interview with Baldwin only vague references were made to the Samuel Memorandum and Bevin asked the Prime Minister to ensure that victimisation didn't take place. But no positive responses were forthcoming, although the Prime Minister later informed the House of Commons of the decision and called the nation to 'work in a spirit of co-operation and put behind us all malice and vindictiveness . . .'[20]

On their return to TUC headquarters, Eccleston Square, Arthur Pugh and Walter Citrine sent telegrams to the trade unions instructing them to order the resumption of work and later a letter, with the details of the Samuel Memorandum, was sent out to all unions. They were held to represent 'sufficient assurances . . . as to the lines upon which a settlement could be reached to justify them terminating the General Strike', a decision taken to enable negotiations to continue.[21] The General Council later justified its position, in June, by suggesting that 'The strike was terminated for one sufficient reason only, namely that in view of the attitude of the Miners' Federation its continuance would have rendered its purpose futile.'[22]

The end of the strike

Why had the strike come to such a swift and unsatisfactory conclusion for the trade unions? The routeway to settlement seems clear. The TUC General Council, never convinced that the General Strike could be prosecuted successfully, had hoped that Samuel would act as a broker for settlement. Once negotiations began with Samuel, and as it became evident that the miners would not compromise on their commitment to wage cuts, it became obvious that the General Council would push for the end of the dispute. The fact is that an agreement with Samuel represented the only way in which an organised retreat from the strike commitment could be made by the General Council.

The Government may well have been equally eager for a settlement but was not prepared to contemplate the possibility of a resumption of negotiations until the strike was over. Indeed, Arthur Steel-Maitland, the Minister of Labour, had made this clear to Samuel:

> Until the necessary orders have been given to withdraw the Strike or unless the Strike has come to an end we cannot as a condition or inducement take part in negotiations in relation to the mining issue . . . [the Government] hold that the General Strike is unconstitutional and illegal. They are bound to take steps to make its repetition impossible. . . . In these circumstances I am sure that the Government will take a view that while they are bound most carefully and most sympathetically to consider the terms of an arrangement which a public man of your responsibility and experience may propose, it is imperative to make it plain that any discussion which you think proper to initiate is not clothed in even a vestige of official character.[23]

Nevertheless, there was much confusion about whether or not the Government would accept Samuel's ideas once the strike was ended. Samuel had explained this position to the TUC Negotiating Committee but it was clear that they felt that his views would carry some weight with Government. Some trade union leaders pinned their hopes on Samuel. Arthur Pugh complained to Samuel that he had been misled:

> It is quite true you made it clear that you had no authority to speak for the Government, but I and my Committee placed implicit faith in yourself. Your standing in the Country, your responsibility and

that of your Colleagues – whom we understood you had consulted – for the recent Report, gave us the conviction that if the strike was called off, the Government would at least offer the Miners to take your Memorandum as a basis for negotiation.[24]

On 22 May, Ernest Bevin, and two other trade-union officials, suggested the same, indicating that they had been led to believe that the Samuel terms would be recognised by the Government.[25] Indeed, Bevin informed his union officers and branches that:

> With regard to the calling off of the strike you may take it from me that we, who were not on the Negotiating Committee, were assured that the Samuel Document would be accepted, that the lock-out notices would be withdrawn and that methods of resumption would be discussed forthwith; and when these assurances had been given us, we naturally felt we had accomplished the purpose for which the strike was called.[26]

Yet it is difficult to believe that Bevin and some of the others who were not on the Negotiating Committee did not know what was going on.

As for the Government, there has been much speculation at what would have happened if the miners had accepted the Samuel Memorandum. Would it have forced the Government to accept the agreement, as the TUC was later to suggest? Symons, Bullock and Crook all feel that the Government would have been obliged to do so.[27] Scheps suggests not, for to have done so would have condoned 'the one idea which they had declared unthinkable – the cancellation of the General Strike by a process of bargaining'.[28] Indeed, Scheps may well be right for it is most unlikely that the Government could afford to lose face as it had done in July 1925. All the evidence is that it refused to negotiate a settlement under the threat of a strike.

In the final analysis, the General Council seems to have convinced itself, against the advice it was being given, that the Government would honour an arrangement to which it had not been a party. As Phillips suggests:

> The endorsement of the Samuel Memorandum by the General Council, it must be concluded, was largely due to their psychological need to believe in it. Throughout the course of the stoppage they had deceived themselves in the same fashion – crediting

Baldwin with conciliatory intentions which had been restrained by other ministers; assuming, at least in the case of the Negotiating Committee, that the miners had undergone a change of heart on the question of wage reductions; hoping that the strike could be ended without disturbance or friction. The adoption of this settlement was part of the same pattern of self-induced optimism.[29]

Conclusion

The settlement of the dispute appears to have arisen from the General Council's fear of challenging the Constitution and the Government. It had committed itself to supporting the miners but, from the beginning, as Citrine reflected many times, there was little prospect of victory. The Samuel Memorandum formed the one possibility of an orderly retreat from conflict but the self-induced confidence in it could not hide the surrender which it represented and the fact that the Government did not endorse it. The calling off of the General Strike was a disaster for the General Council, but that did not necessarily mean that the trade union movement was set back a generation. Indeed, despite the actions which were taken against it, it was remarkably more successful after 1926 than it had been before.

Notes

1 Cook, *Nine Days*, pp. 17–18.
2 *Ibid.*, pp. 18–24.
3 *Workers' Bulletin*, 13 May 1926.
4 *Hansard*, 13 May 1926.
5 *Ibid.*, 3 May 1926.
6 *British Gazette*, 5 May 1926, also quoted in Crook, *General Strike*, p. 401.
7 *Hansard*, 3 May 1926.
8 *Ibid.*, 6 May 1926; Sir John Simon, *Three Speeches on the General Strike*, London, 1926, p. 47.
9 *The Times*, 9 May 1926.
10 *Ibid.*, 11 May 1926.
11 Phillips, *General Strike*, pp. 183–8; Cab 23/52/26 (26) and 28 (28).
12 *British Worker*, 10 May 1926.
13 Citrine, *Men and Work*, p. 187.
14 Look at the Document Section.

15 Cook, *Nine Days*, p. 18; Postgate, Wilkinson and Horrabin, *Workers' History*, pp. 9, 80–3.

16 Citrine, *Men and Work*, pp. 194–5.

17 General Council, *Mining Dispute*, 1927, p. 21.

18 Cook, *Nine Days*, p.15.

19 Citrine, 'Mining Crisis and National Strike', 11 May 1926; Citrine, *Men and Work*, pp. 200–1.

20 *Hansard*, 12 May 1926.

21 Look at Document Section.

22 TUC General Council, *Report to the Conference of Executives of Affiliated Unions, June 25, 1926*, TUC, London, 1926, p. 26.

23 Jones, *Whitehall Diaries*, p. 42; Cab 23/52 27 (26).

24 Samuel Papers (House of Lords Record Office) A/66, Pugh to Samuel, 18 May 1926.

25 *Observer*, 23 May 1926.

26 Bevin Papers, Series C, box 5, C2/3/34, 28 May 1926.

27 Symons, *General Strike*, p. 222; Bullock, *Bevin*, I, p. 343; Crook, *General Strike*, pp. 434–5.

28 A. Scheps, 'Trade Unions and Government, 1925–27, with special reference to the General Strike', Oxford University D.Phil., 1972, p. 347.

29 Phillips, *General Strike*, p. 240.

5

The return to work and the problem of the coal lock-out

The ending of the General Strike created confusion not least because this action was initially represented as being a success for the TUC General Council. Indeed, Walter Citrine its Acting Secretary, sent letters to the secretaries of all the affiliated trade unions and trades councils stating that:

> The General Council, through the magnificent support and soli darity of the Trade Union Movement has obtained assurances that a settlement of the Mining Problem can be secured which justifies them in bringing the general stoppage to an end. . . .
>
> The Government had declared that under no circumstances could negotiations take place until the general strike had been terminated, but the General Council feel as a result of the conversations with Sir Herbert Samuel and the proposals which are embodied in the correspondence and documents which are enclosed that sufficient assurances had been obtained as to the lines upon which a sufficient settlement could be reached to justify them in terminating the General Strike. . . .[1]

Yet it soon became obvious that the Samuel Memorandum was not to be the basis of a settlement in mining, that there had been no guarantees against the victimisation of those workers who had been called out, although Baldwin had hoped that there would be no 'vindictiveness and malice'[2], and that the calling off of the General Strike had been a disaster of mammoth proportions for the TUC – even if its loss of credibility and respect was to have a more immediate than long-term impact.

Local reaction

At first there was both elation and shock at the calling off of the dispute. In Bradford, it was felt that a victory had been secured. *The Bradford Pioneer* stated that:

> We do not say the Government has been defeated by the General Strike, for it was directed against the Government. But we do say that its object (has) been gained, and that after all the stir and excitement, the inconvenience and the lying we are back to where we wished to be, with the miners' case under negotiation.[3]

Elsewhere, there were victory celebrations. On 16 May, at Summerfield Park, Birmingham, Oswald Mosley announced to the assembled trade unionists that 'they had whipped the Government'.[4] Yet in other areas there was grave concern. At Hull there was 'Alarm – fear – despair – a victorious army disarmed and handed over to its enemies.' At Wakefield 'The spirit was magnificent, and consternation and dismay prevailed when the news that the strike was called off had been confirmed.'[5] Sheffield Central Dispute Committee was one of the most critical, passing a resolution condemning the action of the General Council, castigating the 'surrender being unconditional', and demanding an immediate investigation into the circumstances which led to the end of the strike.[6] In effect, then, there was tremendous confusion and bitterness in the wake of the General Council's decision to terminate the strike. However, within days it was clear to all that the General Council's decision was something of a debacle.

The General Council had left it to the individual unions to organise a return to work and the euphoria and misgivings quickly turned to alarm when they realised that this was not the victory which had been expected and once it became obvious that the employers were, at least initially, attempting to cash in on the collapse of the strike in order to root out trade union officials and members from their works. The Admiralty dockyards, Conservative-dominated local authorities, railway companies and many other employers attempted to force the returning strikers to agree that they would never break their contracts again and, in some cases, attempted to impose non-unionisation as a condition of employment. Phillips, Renshaw, and Morris, have all pointed to the high level of victimisation that occurred and, indeed, they are right to do so. But what is also evident is that this muscular action by employers varied enormously from region to region. In some areas attempts at victimisation lasted as long as it took for the trade unionists to threaten the continuation of the strike whilst in other areas it took a more protracted form.

The picture emerging from the local strike centres is not at all clear. In Cheltenham, the Tory Council had the Tram Service announce that 'Old employees can return on the same wages, but must work longer hours.' In addition, the following was posted:

> Notice to all men who dismissed themselves from their work. Kindly turn in all uniforms and all property of the Company within the next twelve hours and collect insurance cards. Applications for re-employment will be considered only from non-union men.[7]

In fact, as with the situation of the Gloucester dockers, the employers eventually backed down, although they insisted that the railwaymen should sign a document 'making them personally liable for a breach of contract'.[8] Indeed, Williams makes the point that 'Compared with a number of other places in the country, such as Glasgow, Barnsley, Doncaster and Leeds, there was little bitterness shown by either side during or after the strike in North Gloucestershire.'[9]

The situation does not appear to have been much different in the North East, one of the areas which most strongly supported the General Strike. Tony Mason suggests that the London and North Eastern Railway did indicate that it would 'give preference to those who remained at work', and other companies followed suit.[10] Yet he declares that there was 'some victimisation – probably less than might have been expected'.[11] There also appears to have been little victimisation in other areas such as Devon. And, as already indicated, the situation was somewhat similar in Bradford.

Yet in some other major industrial centres the situation was quite different. In Glasgow 368 of the 5,000 tramwaymen were suspended or dismissed and at Newport 300 volunteers were kept on at the expense of the members of the General and Municipal Workers' Union. Brighton Council also forced its tramway staff to leave the Transport and General Workers' Union.[12] Matters seem to have been equally bad on Merseyside, Birmingham, York – areas where transport unions, dockers and

91

other groups were amongst the most important occupational groups.

Initially, matters appear to have been settled reasonably amicably in the Liverpool area, for the Merseyside Council of Action informed its supporters that:

> The Council has now ascertained that a large number of employers and Employers' Federations (including the Dock Board, Shipowners, and the Liverpool Cotton Association) have agreed to carry out the resumption of work policy on the old agreements and no victimization on either side.
>
> The Council feel that this is a practical expression of the Prime Minister's statement that 'neither malice nor vindictiveness should be exhibited' and it is to be hoped that it will be regarded as an example to be followed by all employers on the Merseyside and elsewhere.[13]

The reality was quite otherwise for there was a slow return to work on Merseyside as the men fought to get back to work on the old terms. The railway unions held out against the proposed national settlement which insisted that the General Strike was a 'wrongful act', the men at Clover Claytons, the Birkenhead Ship Repairers, downed tools only three hours after they had been re-engaged once they realised that the railwaymen were not back. The dockers stayed out for another six days and it was many months before the tugboatmen and floating crane operators were taken back by the Mersey Docks and Harbour Board.[14] Indeed, Liverpool was the only port in the country where these groups were victimised. The Conservative-dominated tramway undertakings of Merseyside were also determined to make an example of the strikers and eight months after the strike there were still sixty tramwaymen who had not been re-instated. In Birkenhead, the tramway company had taken on volunteers plus some forty permanent employees and managed to run the buses, though not the trams. All the strikers were given notice but after deputations and two days of strikes by the dockers the Council agreed to reinstate the 380 strikers as jobs became available. On 27 May, thirty-one were still out of work and some police protection was required when the trams were restarted. In milling, however, there was more protracted conflict as volunteers ran the mills from 11 to 20 May.[15]

The situation was similar in York, where the ending of the

strike had been greeted with disbelief and distress. The railway companies intimated that the workers would not necessarily get their old jobs back and so, on 13 May, the three main railway unions indicated their intention to keep the dispute going. They placed more pickets than ever before on the stations and worked with other groups of workers who had not returned. After several days struggle, and agreements by the three national railway unions on humiliating terms with the employers, the men gradually drifted back to work with most of their old conditions guaranteed.[16] At Nottingham, the situation was little better. In West Bridgeford, fifty per cent of the transport department had their jobs filled with blackleg labour and four members of the United Builders, who had struck at the Raleigh Cycle Company, were not re-employed.[17] Finally, in Birmingham employers supported the policy of unconditional surrender advocated by Neville Chamberlain, MP. With the exception of Joseph Lucas Ltd, who gave a message of goodwill to the 500 returning brassworkers and engineers, and paid them for the time occupied by the meeting, many concerns forced men to return on the minimum wage.[18] Avery's and Tagy's dismissed strikers who had not reported back and accepted only individual applications for reinstatement.[19] The Engineering and Allied Employers' Federation refused to give the engineering unions any assurances of continued employment upon re-engagement whilst the railwaymen were informed that they could return in order of seniority and grade and on the understanding that they were not relieved of any of the responsibilities of their breach of contract.[20]

If the local and regional picture was varied this was not so in the national negotiations between employers and trade unions. The Government imposed penalties on its own workers who had come out on strike, some of them forfeiting a year's pension or gratuity and those guilty of intimidation being dismissed. It was suggested that their trade-union representatives should be forced to acknowledge that the stoppage was 'a wrongful act'. Such conditions were imposed in the Admiralty. As already indicated, the road transport workers were pressured by employers and one of the leading London bus companies, Thomas Tilling's, withdrew recognition from the Transport and General Workers' Union. Indeed, nationally, about 1,900 busmen and tramwaymen lost their jobs through victimisation.[21]

The printing employers also proved intransigent in their opposition to the strikers. They united to eliminate trade union organisation in Scotland, and the *Manchester Guardian* formed its own house union. The Fleet Street proprietors also took the offensive but eventually came to terms with their employees on 20 May, upon getting the unions to agree that there would be no more attempts to deal with the contents of the newspapers. Railway employers seem to have varied from place to place – some threatening to reduce entitlements and others attempting to force workers to sign statements indicating their willingness to refrain from further strike action. But the railway workers remained on strike on 13 May and C. T. Cramp wrote to the general managers of the major companies calling for the unconditional reinstatement of all workers: 'very large numbers of Railwaymen have definitely refused to take up duty under the conditions which obtain, and it is only right that I should make it very clear that I cannot hope to influence them to speedily take up their duties under the present conditions'.[22] Eventually a compromise was arranged in which in return for reinstatement, the guaranteed week was suspended, the unions acknowledged that they had done a 'wrongful act', agreed that the employers could claim for damages and promised not to strike in advance of negotiations.

In other industries the repercussions were much less serious. As Frank Wilkinson has suggested in his detailed study of collective bargaining in the steel industry. 'Despite this lapse during the General Strike the industry maintained its reputation for peacefully resolving its own wage disputes during the 1920s'.[23] The industry was in fact marked by an unusual degree of industrial peace and the General Strike does not appear to have fundamentally altered its pattern of industrial negotiations.

How are we to assess these developments? Quite clearly there was serious victimisation in some regions and some industries, but compared with the impact of the industrial action of both miners and the TUC in increasing unemployment from about one million to one and two-third millions between 24 April and 31 May, the post-strike action of the employers was little more than token action to attempt to ensure that trade unionists noted their future obligations to work within negotiated agreements. Most employers were happy to return to normal working conditions and, subsequently, were quite happy to aim towards an understanding with trade unions. In the immediate wake of the cessation of General Strike hostilities, however, this was not true of the coal-mine owners.

The coal mining lock-out, April–November 1926

The coal mining dispute, the cause of the General Strike, lasted for almost seven months until the miners were forced back to work on the employers' terms. During that period both the Miners' Federation and the coal owners remained intractable, the latter seeing the possibility of weakening the influence of the MFGB.

Herbert Smith was rigidly opposed to settlement and made it almost impossible for Cook, who favoured compromise, to settle the dispute. Paul Davies has recently revealed the extent to which Cook went to negotiate secretly with Seebohm Rowntree and Walter Layton on 2 July 1926 and with Sir Stephen Demetriadi, the Chairman of the London Chamber of Commerce towards the end of July. Neither effort at negotiations achieved a great deal, and both focused upon the acceptance of the Samuel Commission Report and the processes by which wage levels, the reorganisation of industry and longer hours, would be determined. But in the end they remained 'covert, single-handed negotiations', of which the MFGB seem to have known little until 1928.[24]

In this unpropitious climate there seemed little prospect of settlement, and it is not surprising that the Government's attempt to intervene never stood a chance of acceptance. The miners and Baldwin met on 13 May when they informed him that they were not interested in Samuel's proposals, much to the relief of a Government which was not particularly interested in settlement on that basis.[25] At the same time Steel-Maitland, the Minister of Labour, met the coal owners who were equally unhelpful.[26] On the 14 May the Government outlined its proposals for settlement, suggesting compulsory arbitration, the decision of which would be imposed by a Wages Board within three weeks of its establishment with, in the meantime, an interim wage reduction operating within the context of a restructuring of the coal industry. It also offered a temporary and small subsidy to ease the wage cuts. Although many of the points interested the miners there were sufficient omissions and concerns, particularly the possibility of a 10 per cent cut in wages, which discouraged the special conference of the miners from accepting the proposal on 20 May.[27] The mine-owners were equally emphatic in their resistance to the Government's proposals, not least because they included the need to re-organise the coal industry, along the lines of the Samuel Commission which the Government had accepted as a basis for discussion. Consequently, the Government effectively withdrew from negotiations although Baldwin did meet the miners and Bevin at the end of May when he urged them to accept longer hours: 'put it to them that "hours" was the way out. If they went on with the strike they would be beaten. I did not move them'.[28]

The fact is that the Government had become convinced that the raising of hours of work was the way out of the dispute. Steel-Maitland and others had suggested this in May and, even though the miners rejected the suggestion, newspaper reports and a variety of advice influenced the Government to feel that if the Seven Hours Act was suspended for five years then miners would accept the eight-hour day and the opportunity it provided for a settlement.[29] Then, on 15 June, the Cabinet decided to suspend the Seven Hours Act for five years and enacted this decision in early July, accompanied by a Mining Industry Act which implemented some measures of reorganisation.[30] This united the TUC General Council and the MFGB, who might otherwise have been embroiled in internecine conflict as a result of A. J. Cook's recently published pamphlet *The Nine Days*. Yet such harmony was brief-lived as a result of the General Council's decision, in mid-July, not to impose the embargo on coal imports which the MFGB had requested.

It was not until early September, faced with signs of a return to work in some districts such as Nottingham, that the MFGB decided to re-open negotiations for a 'new national agreement with a view to a reduction of labour costs'.[31] Immediately, Churchill and the Cabinet's coal committee pursued this possibility of a solution, meeting with the Mining Association which refused to consider the establishment of a national agreement. Eventually the Cabinet put forward a plan, drafted by Cunliffe-

Lister, to establish a wage tribunal with power to revise, on appeal, district agreements on an eight-hour basis, but this proved unacceptable to the coal owners and was rejected by a majority of almost 700,000 miners.[32]

Over the next few weeks an intricate array of posturing took place, with the miners reasserting their original position and the General Council attempting to intervene to settle the dispute. However, the miners and the General Council were still faced with the Cabinet Coal Committee decision to support district negotiations covering hours and wages. This, and all its ramifications, was offered by the executive to the districts and a vote led to its rejection by 460,806 votes to 313,200.[33] The national conference of the MFGB therefore ordered its constituents to make their own terms, consistent as far as possible with agreed national standards. At this point the miners began to drift back to work on varied terms. All the workers returned on a seven and a half hours day in Yorkshire whilst longer hours and wage reductions were imposed in South Wales, Scotland and the North-East. In Nottinghamshire, those workers who had returned to work under George Spencer's breakaway union were given a four shillings per week wage increase.

Conclusion

There was no doubt that the collapse of the General Strike and the capitulation of the miners in the coal lock-out were devastating results for the British trade union movement – earning the General Council some obloquy. The prestige, effectiveness and membership of the trade union movement appeared to suffer in the short term. Nevertheless, the trade unions were not destroyed and continued to mount an effective block to the control of the employers in industry – where co-operation and understanding was still a marked feature of industrial life.

Notes

1   Letter from the TUC General Council to all Secretaries of Affiliated Trade Unions and for the Information of Trade Councils and Strike Committees, 12 May 1926, to be found in many collections of trades council and trade union documents. Also in TUC Archives;

K. Laybourn, *British Trade Unionism c 1770–1990: A Reader in History*, Sutton, Stroud, 1991, pp. 149–50. Also look at Document Section.

2   *Hansard*, 12 May 1926.

3   *Bradford Pioneer*, 14 May 1926.

4   Hastings, 'Birmingham', p. 268.

5   Farman, *General Strike*, p. 237.

6   Central Disputes Committee, Sheffield, 13 May 1926, West Yorkshire Archives, Bradford, 56D80/10/2, 89.

7   Williams, 'Gloucestershire', p. 210.

8   Crook, *General Strike*, p. 450, quoting *Gloucestershire Strike Bulletin*, 13 May 1926.

9   Williams, 'Gloucestershire', p. 212.

10   Mason, *North East*, p. 91, quoting *Northern Echo*, 13 May 1926.

11   *Ibid.*, p. 96.

12   Phillips, *General Strike*, p. 245.

13   Special Bulletin issued by the Merseyside Council of Action, 13 May 1926, signed by W. H. Boston (Chairman) and W. H. Barton (Secretary), Liverpool Record Office and copies in possession of Keith Laybourn.

14   Baines and Bean, 'Merseyside', pp. 261–3.

15   *Ibid.*, p. 264.

16   Hills, *York*, p. 24.

17   Wyncoll, 'Nottingham', p. 179.

18   Hastings, 'Birmingham', p. 268.

19   *Ibid.*, p. 270.

20   *Birmingham Post*, 14 May 1926.

21   General Council, 129, 13/7/1, Bevin to Firth, 29 May; TGWU GEC minutes, Report of Sub-committee on the General Strike.

22   NUR/ GS, Head Office Circulars.

23   F. Wilkinson, 'Collective Bargaining in the Steel Industry in the 1920s', *Essays in Labour History 1918–1939*, Croom Helm, Beckenham, 1977, p. 103.

24   Davies, *Cook*, pp. 11–14, 194–207.

25   Cab 27/318 Rcc (26) 38, 13 May 1926.

26   Memorandum for the PM on Meeting with mine-owners, Thursday 13 May 1926, in the Steel-Maitland Papers.

27   Miners' Federation of Great Britain, 1926, p. 445.

28   Jones, *Whitehall Diary*, 31 May 1926, p. 60.

29   Cab 27/316 RCC 26/11, 20 May 1926; *Daily Mail*, 28 May 1926; Amery to Baldwin, 1 June 1926, Vol. 18, D3, 4a Baldwin Papers.

30   Cab 2 3/53, 38 (26); Scheps, 'Trade Unions and the Government, 1925–27', p. 361.

31   Jones, *Whitehall Diaries*, pp. 68–9.

32 MFGB, EC minutes, 20–21 September and letter of Evan Williams to Winston Churchill, 13 September 1926, quoted in MFGB, Minutes, 1026, pp. 774–5.

33 MFGB, Minutes, 1926, p. 1037.

6

The consequences of the General Strike; a watershed in British industrial relations?

According to the Communist Party of Great Britain:

> The General Council's decision to call off the General Strike is the greatest crime that has ever been permitted, not only against the miners, but against the working class of Great Britain and the whole world. The British workers had aroused the astonishment and admiration of the world by the enthusiasm with which they had entered upon the fight for the miners' standard of living. But instead of responding to this magnificent lead by a call to every section of organised labour to join the fight against the capitalists, the General Council has miserably thrown itself and the miners on the tender mercies of the workers' worst enemies – the Tory Government.[1]

Similar views were expressed by many others, including A. J. Cook who was annoyed, assertive and accusative in his pamphlet *The Nine Days*:

> It seemed that the only desire of some leaders was to call off the General Strike at any cost, without any guarantees for the workers, miners, or others.
>
> By this action of theirs, in 'turning off the power', the miners were left alone in their struggle.
>
> A few days longer and the Government and the capitalist class, financiers, parasites and exploiters, would have been compelled to make peace with the miners. We should thus have secured in the mining industry a settlement which would have redounded to the honour and credit of the British Labour Movement, and would

have been a fitting reward for the solidarity displayed by the workers.[2]

Three points emerge from a distillation of these criticisms: that the General Council betrayed the miners and their rank and file trade union supporters, that the TUC leadership was not committed to the struggle, and that the strike was winnable. The first is debatable, the second is correct, and the third is clearly wrong. None the less, and conflated, they imply that the General Strike represented, in some way, a watershed in British trade union history. Such a view has been put forward, forcibly, by Martin Jacques, a Marxist writer, who suggests that 1926 proved to be a decisive turning point in the development of working-class movements for 'it marked the end of the last great period of working-class militancy and it saw a massive shift in outlook and orientation of the trade-union movement.'[3] He maintains that trade unions were on the offensive between 1918 and 1926, even though 'Black Friday' and the economic depression had undermined their combativity and moved their power base from the rank and file to the trade union leadership – a clearly retrogressive step. Yet, apparently:

> These tendencies did not, however, become decisive until after the General Strike. Thus between 1921 and 1926 the mood of key sections of industrial workers remained militant, combative and cohesive. At the same time, the trade union movement was, within limits, willing and prepared to fight. Thus, while the appearance of mass unemployment had an important impact on the trade union movement it did not in itself mark a decisive turning point.[4]

Indeed, syndicalist ideas and labourist attitudes were, apparently, used in conjunction to justify industrial action to influence political decisions. This situation changed dramatically after 1926, when the General Strike became a watershed in British trade unionism and British industrial relations.

Alan Bullock, in his informed and perceptive biography of Ernest Bevin, does, from a more right-wing viewpoint, also suggest that the 1926 General Strike acted as 'a turning point'.[5] His view is influenced by the diaries of Beatrice Webb which state that:

For the British trade union movement I see a day of terrible disillusionment. The failure of the General Strike of 1926 will be one of the most significant landmarks in the history of the British working-class. Future historians will, I think, regard it as the death-gasp of that pernicious doctrine of 'workers' control' of public affairs through the trade unions and by the method of direct action.[6]

This view he regards to have been fully justified for 'On the far side of 1926, we enter a different climate of opinion from the turbulent years of the earlier 1920s.'[7] To Bullock, the militancy of the pre-1926 period contrasts with its decline thereafter. And:

The events of 1926 showed Bevin and the other union leaders that there were limits not only to their power but also to the use they could afford to make of it unless they were prepared to risk being carried much further than most meant to go. Industrial action on a national scale was bound to have political and constitutional implications whether intended or not.[8]

In essence, his view is that the unions did not abandon the strike weapon but used it more cautiously from then onwards.

Some other historians have argued a similar line. Renshaw, in particular, considers the General Strike as a decisive turning point, a dividing point between 'the turbulent class politics of the immediate post-war period and the relative quiescent acceptance by Labour of mass unemployment in the late 1920s and the 1930s'.[9] These views, of course, do not accord with those developed by Gordon Phillips and Hugh Clegg, who maintain that the trajectory of trade union history was not altered by the events of 1926 and that the pattern of activity and policy remained in the some grooves after 1926 as they had been before. Trade union leaders had espoused industrial peace after the First World War, a view which has been recently confirmed by Chris Wrigley, and continued to do so after the General Strike. Wrigley in fact writes that 'Among a significant number of trade unionists the experience of wartime cooperation with employers, combined with a distate for the new militancy, reinforced a pre-war taste for joint committees and for the settling of industrial differences within industries without recourse to Whitehall.'[10] In essence, then, the aims of trade unions remained those of their leaders – to create trade union unity, to improve industrial relations and to work with the employers, and even the Government, in actions which would improve the employment situation of the workers. In the end, the distant hope was that in the near future strikes would be rendered almost unnecessary.

The crux of the debate is thus the question – what did the General Strike mean for the trade union movement, British industrial relations and the general pattern of relations between the workers, the employers and the Government? Was it a turning point, or watershed, in British industrial relations, or did it make little impact upon the pre-1926 pattern of events? By and large, the evidence tends to support the views of Clegg and Phillips rather than Jacques, Bullock and Renshaw. Notwithstanding the internecine conflict within trade unionism and the decline of the prestige of the General Council, which the failure of the General Strike engendered, it is, nevertheless, clear that the TUC and the trade union movement remained remarkably intact. In no significant way could the General Strike be considered a turning point or watershed in British industrial history. Indeed, the most obvious point is that trade unionism continued to develop along the same lines as it had done before 1926 and it retained much of its membership despite a modest slippage in the late 1920s and early 1930s. The details of trade union membership are given in item 36 of the document section and what they indicate is that membership was falling from 1921 and that 1926 continued that decline. The coal miners, for instance, declined from 936,653 members in 1921 to 885,789 in 1925, 762,916 in 1926 and 592,379 in 1928. The decline was fairly steady. In other industries, such as building, textiles and shipbuilding the decline was less rapid after 1926 than before and during the 1930s there was often rapid recovery. This meant that in the late 1920s and early 1930s the union density in most industries declined, but this might have occurred in any case as a result of the economic depression.

On balance, it would appear that the trajectory of trade union membership was determined more by the economy than by the fate of industrial disputes, even one so large as 1926, though the fate of the 1919–21 strikes, many of which were defeats, and the onset of mass unemployment from 1921–2 predetermined a difficult and defensive period overall.

Also, in respect of syndicalism and the demand for workers'

control it is clear that what little influence they had before 1926 had declined altogether. The General Strike revealed once and for all that pure industrial strategy would not work and that the trade union movement had better get on to the Labour Party train rather than fooling about with the ultimate deterrent – the General Strike. In the late 1920s and the early 1930s Ernest Bevin took the trade union movement more firmly into the Labour Party than it had ever been before. There were more trade-union sponsored Labour Party candidates than previously and a greater willingness to operate within the joint Labour Party and TUC structures.

The reckoning

Ben Tillett informed Sir Herbert Samuel, on the eve of the end of the dispute, that 'We shall be told we have betrayed the miners. We will get it in the neck for sure.'[11] Indeed, within days of the end of the dispute deputations were sent to London to meet the leading figures of the General Council to establish what went wrong.[12] The fact that the TUC was reluctant to organise a boycott of imported coal exacerbated a tense situation. Yet, in general, the criticism within trade union ranks was somewhat mooted. Even amongst the miners only Cook expressed his disgust in a highly contentious pamphlet, *The Nine Days*, which was criticised for its bias and was subjected to some constraints. Indeed, the MFGB did not issue its official criticism until January 1927 when it accused the General Council of failing to carry out its commitment to their cause.

The General Council wished to rebut any charges of betrayal at the earliest opportunity, but it was decided not to hold a proposed conference of union executives for 25 June 1926. Instead it attempted to maintain a rule of silence at least until the mining dispute was over, a situation which the MFGB generally accepted. However, total silence could not be maintained, as became obvious at the TUC Conference held at Bournmouth, 6 – 11 September 1926. On this occasion, the TUC was advocating public control as the solution to the problems of the mining industry on the principle of 'The Mines for the Nation'.[13] In a neutral statement, designed to show respect for the support given to the miners by all trade unionists and yet to disabuse anyone of the idea that the General Strike was revolutionary, Arthur Pugh, in his presidential address, stated that:

> It will be fatal to the future welfare of this country and destructive of all our hopes of peaceable progress, if that great and spontaneous demonstration of working-class solidarity, so generous in its readiness to run risks and make sacrifices on behalf of others, so inspiring, as a revelation to the true spirit of Trade Union brotherhood, is regarded as the outcome of a sort of evil conspiracy of a few agitators meeting in Eccleston Square. It has been so misinterpreted. Nothing can be more dangerous than to proceed upon an assumption so false and so perverse.[14]

He also added that the General Strike revealed the trade unions to be democratic in their methods.[15] None the less, some minor controversy ensued when John Bromley, the ASLEF secretary, was shouted down by the miners and the left-wing delegates in response to an earlier attack he had made upon the miners. There was also an attempt by the Communists to pass a motion objecting to the suggestion that the debate about the strike be delayed to the deferred conference of executives, but it won only three quarters of a million votes and failed to get even the miners' support.[16]

Nevertheless, the general charges of the miners against the TUC began to emerge. There were six main accusations: that the TUC had made no effective preparations for the General Strike; that it had not sought the authority of the conference of trade union executives for approval; that it failed to protect the workers from victimisation; that the MFGB had not been fully consulted of the General Council's negotiations with the Government and Samuel; that the Samuel Memorandum had been accepted without any Government guarantees of acceptance; and, lastly, that the TUC's willingness to accept a wage reduction ran against the resolution which had empowered the General Council to call a strike.[17] The TUC rejected these specific charges at a Conference of Trade Union Executives on 20 and 21 January 1927.[18] It suggested that elaborate preparations were unnecessary given the limited power and resources of the General Council, that it had been given full powers and procedural delays were unnecessary, that individual unions had the responsibility to prevent victimisation, that the miners effectively made consultations futile since they would not agree to negotiations and a collective policy, that if the miners had accepted the Samuel Memorandum the Government would have had to accept it, and that a wage reduction had been agreed as a practical basis for compromise.

Many of these responses were debatable. Obviously, the General Council had been given responsibility for the dispute, but it was obligated to defend the existing employment conditions of the miners. Also, the suggestion that the Government would have been obligated to accept the Samuel Memorandum, had the miners' accepted it, has already been shown to be spurious, given that the Government was committed to rejecting negotiations until the General Strike was called off. In other words, the Government could not have accepted the Samuel Memorandum as a basis for ending the General Strike.

What was even more significant is what was kept out of the discussion. The General Council in fact kept quiet on some aspects of its negotiations and clearly failed to acquit itself of the charge of betrayal. Yet most trade unions were happy to let that ride as they also felt that the miners had failed to accept collective responsibility in the whole affair. On balance then, whilst the miners criticised the General Council for its lack of commitment to defending their wages and conditions the General Council criticised the miners for their unbending attitudes in the face of possible compromises which would have served their cause better than industrial defeat.

The Trades Dispute Act, 1927

The relatively sedate nature of the potentially destructive and damaging debate between the TUC and the miners was, in some ways, determined by the fact that the Government had declared its intention to take legislative action to curb trade union power. Indeed, such a commitment pre-dated the General Strike for Baldwin's Conservative Government had come to power on the basis of tackling the political levy by which trade unionists provided money for the Labour Party. Indeed, there was pressure to push forward with a Bill to change the basis of the political levy, although Baldwin opposed it on the grounds that it would harm class co-operation. In the end the Government, which had initially set up a Cabinet Committee to deal with it, passed an amendment through the House of Commons which effectively blocked the threatened private members' bill:

> This House while approving the principle of political liberty embodied in the Trade Union (Political Fund) Bill, is of opinion that a measure of such far-reaching importance should not be introduced as Private Member's Bill.[19]

The situation changed somewhat as a result of the General Strike. As a result the demand for control of the political levy revived alongside the demand for the control of sympathetic strike action.

A revival of interest in trade union legislation occurred when there were rumblings within the Cabinet of the need to set up a Cabinet Committee to consider future trade union legislation. This occurred shortly after 'Red Friday' but became more meaningful after the General Strike, when it was felt that there was a need to make the Astbury Judgment law and a need to prevent the victimisation by trade unions of those who had continued to work. Some Government opinion also felt that there should be compulsory secret ballots before strikes could take place. In this climate, a Cabinet Committee was set up to deal with the complex problem of trade union legislation.[20]

The final Bill took shape over about nine months and reflected the interests of various members in the Cabinet and the pressure groups who operated upon them. It was published in March 1927, had its second reading in May and became law on 29 July, despite the comment of Lord Reading that its language 'is more vague, more indefinite, more lacking in precision than any Bill or Act of Parliament he had dealt with'.[21] Three of the eight main clauses dealt with the prohibition of general strikes, one suggested the need for trade unionists to opt into paying the political levy, rather than to opt out, and there were sanctions against some trade unions being linked to the TUC as well as further restrictions on picketing.

The new act was in fact kaleidoscopic in the interests which it brought together and lacked real direction and coherence. Its most important impact was to reduce the number of trade unionists paying the levy for the Labour Party from 3,200,000 in 1927 to 2,000,000 in 1929.[22] As far as industrial relations was concerned it provoked only one or two court cases and by and large its purely industrial measures were ignored, and the act was finally withdrawn in 1946. The relative insignificance of the act belies the antagonism which it engendered within Labour ranks. The National Trade Union Defence Committee was formed in April 1927 and organised about 1,100 meetings throughout the country, but the impact was limited and the action proved unnecessary.[23]

The consequences of the General Strike

The General Strike has been seen as a watershed by some historians.[24] They point to a variety of evidence to support their contention. First, they suggest that the General Strike caused a rapid decline in trade union membership, from 5,219,000 in 1926 to 4,392,000 by 1933.[25] This, evidently, was a product of the victimisation of the strikers and possibly the result of a loss of support for the trade union movement rather than due to the economic conditions, which were reasonably good in 1927 and 1928. The decline in union funds of trade unions from £12,500,000 at the beginning of 1926 to less than £8,500,000 by the end may also have been a contributory factor to the declining appeal and effectiveness of trade unionism.[26] The declining demand for workers' control and the dramatic drop in the number of days lost due to strikes, ignoring 1926, from almost eight millions in 1925 to 1,174,000 in 1927, also seems to provide evidence of a toothless trade union movement on the retreat.[27] The negotiations between the employers and the TUC, known as the Mond-Turner talks, which took place in the late 1920s, are also used in a major way to provide proof positive of the change which had overcome the trade union movement.

According to Jacques the General Council, in calling off the General Strike, had rejected the notion of the idea of using a general strike or mass industrial action to win its cause. The General Council had come to accept that capitalism was not coming to a quick end, that they had to work within the system to win rights for their members, and accordingly went forward with the Mond-Turner talks. And it is true that Citrine maintained that:

> the unions should actively participate in a concerted effort to raise industry to its highest efficiency by developing the most scientific

methods of production, eliminating harmful restrictions, removing cause of friction and avoidable conflict, and promoting the
largest possible output so as to provide a rising standard of life and
continuously improving conditions of employment.[28]

Jacques notes that there were four main changes in the
ideology of the trade union movement after 1926. The first was
the move from an offensive and defensive policy towards one
directed towards collaboration with employers to achieve
economic recovery. The second was a transfer from the idea that
wage-labour had exclusive common interests, to the wider con-
ception that wage-labour and employers had common interests.
As Bevin reflected at the 1927 TUC Congress 'the management
side has a good deal in common with ourselves'.[29] Thirdly, a new
idea emerged which viewed change as being longer and more
evolutionary and blurred the 'nature of socialist objectives'.
Fourthly, there was a move from industrial to political spheres, in
other words the effective abandonment of industrial action for
political purposes.

Yet Jacques's views are coloured by his Marxist perspective and
he bends the stick too far. For instance, as Wrigley and others
have suggested, there was a strong tendency towards industrial
collaboration well before 1926, a view which challenges the first
two of Jacques's charges. The TUC attitude towards industrial
relations was also, essentially, long-term and evolutionary. It is
also not clear that the TUC had the view that industrial action
could be used for political change. Many of its leaders had
rejected such ideas throughout the early 1920s and the General
Council was most insistent that the General Strike was an industrial dispute in support of the miners and not a threat to the
constitution. As already indicated, such a view was held before
and during, and not just after, the General Strike.

Critics of this perspective have stressed the continuity rather
than the discontinuity of trade union history and the pattern of
industrial relations. Their counter suggestion is that, apart from
the normal reflex actions of a movement under threat, the
thinking, actions, policies and attitudes of the trade union movement did not change in any meaningful or long-term way as a
result of the General Strike. Indeed, Clegg goes as far as to
suggest that the wage reduction after the General Strike were

much less than those which had occurred before the strike – a contentious view given that the depression itself was, at least between 1927 and 1929, less pronounced than it was in the early 1920s. What evidence is there, then, for these counter views and to what extent do they undermine the watershed hypothesis? Briefly, evidence suggests little changed in the long-term attitude of the Government, employers and the trade unions.

As for the Government, it did not alter in any fundamental way the direction it had assumed before 1926. It was committed to introducing legislation to deal with the issue of the political levy before the General Strike but was reluctantly forced into imposing legislation upon sympathetic strike action which it, and subsequent governments, barely attempted to enforce. It has already been demonstrated that the *pot pourri* of measures introduced by the Trades Dispute Act carried little weight, since the Government's main aim was to improve industrial relations. Also, one has to remember that successive post-war governments had, since 1918, sought to maintain reasonably good industrial relations despite the downward movement of wage rates and had, by and large, succeeded in doing so. Indeed, the Baldwin Government had made a determined attempt to solve the wool and worsted textile dispute in 1925, with some success and with Arthur Steel-Maitland, the Minister of Labour, well to the fore.[30]

As for the employers, many were only too glad to get back to good relations with their workforce, particularly after the end of the coal strike which caused severe power shortages and a significant rise in unemployment.[31] As already indicated, the employers in the iron and steel industries were happy to return to pre-1926 industrial relations and, despite some problems amongst the transport workers and the dockers, industrial relations remained good in a number of industries. This type of theme emerges from an important article by G. W. McDonald who has examined the role of British industry in 1926. His main theme is that the coal owners, and their industrial allies, were determined in their opposition to the Samuel Commission, and the Government, on the issue of the reorganisation of the British coal industry and resistance to idea of coal-marketing boards. They controlled the events of 1926 but with a loss of 162 million days due to strikes (146 million in the coal industry), the decline of coal exports from £54 millions to £20,500,000, and the consequent knock-on effect to other industries, particularly iron and steel, it is not surprising that in the wake of the disputes other ideas began to emerge. Sir Alfred Mond had already advocated a softer approach with the trade unions than the coal owners had wanted and the Trades Dispute and Trade Union Act of 1927 was vague and ineffective in comparison with the radical revision of the 1906 Trades Dispute Act and the reduction of trade union power which the hardliners had demanded. McDonald, in effect, suggests that the employers were divided and that after 1926 a softer attitude began to emerge from some sections of the employers. Many were happy to see the number of strike days lost, which had been about eight millions in 1925 and 162 millions in 1926, fall to 1,174,000 in 1927 and 1,388,000 in 1928 before rising again to pre-1926 levels between 1929 and 1932, owing to rising unemployment and wage cuts.[32]

As far as the trade union movement and the TUC were concerned, one does not detect any significant change of direction in the industrial policy they were pursuing. The TUC remained committed to strengthening and co-ordinating the action of trade unionists. At the 1927 TUC congress it was stated, by the President, that:

> This Congress will consider the necessary steps to be taken to adapt the Trade Union Movement to the new conditions created by this Act of Parliament. Congress, I know, will be wise in its decisions. But let me say this: whatever methods it may be possible to agree upon – even though they be of the tamest character in compliance with and abject submission of this tyrannical Act, if that be conceivable – the matter does not end there. There are forces in society stronger than ourselves, those very forces which brought the Union Movement to birth and caused its growth in spite of continuous oppression and persecution, which shaped its destiny and transformed it into the powerful, widespread, and all-embracing movement that it is today – these forces cannot be shackled by legislation.[33]

This may be regarded as the bravado expected by a presidential address to the TUC but it had more substance than might have been expected, given that most major trade union organisations lost members between 1926 and 1928, and that overall trade union membership fell from 5,219,000 in 1926 to 4,806,000 in

1928.[34] Clearly, many unions lost a significant number of their members in the immediate wake of the General Strike but most, except for the miners and the iron and steel workers, managed to retain their membership reasonably well thereafter and trade union membership began to increase rapidly from 1933 onwards. In other words, trade union membership was not massively or permanently damaged as a result of the General Strike; it had in fact fallen more sharply in the early 1920s. Part of the reason was, as H. A. Clegg suggested, due to the fact that:

> The aftermath of the general strike might have given the employers a convenient opportunity to carry through such an attack; but it did not happen. No considerable group of workers, apart from the miners, suffered an extension of agreed working hours either in 1926 or 1927.[35]

Indeed, he adds that without the changes in the pay of miners the average index of wages would have remained the same in 1926 and 1927. And since there was economic stability there was no need for employers to get into a conflict with the workers.

Indeed in the late 1920s there was an almost unprecedented industrial peace. Whether this was because of the relative stability of the economy or the desire for industrial peace after the General Strike is not easy to establish. Yet, it is clear that the employers were as keen as the trade unions to cultivate a better climate for industrial relations. And since the trade unions were still determined to protect their members, in whatever ways were available, it made sense for both sides of industry to work within a mutually acceptable framework.

Certainly, from 1927 onwards the trade union movement appeared to be working towards improving their relationship with employers, along the lines which had already been developed in the immediate post-war years, although the idea of an industrial alliance between trade unions and against employers was to be abandoned. The General Strike had revealed the limits of industrial alliances just as it had revealed to employers the dangers of mass confrontation. As already suggested, Walter Citrine had outlined the basis of a new relationship in his article 'The Next Step in Industrial Relations' and the view emerged that the General Council would be part of a National Industrial Council alongside representatives of the

Confederation of Employers' Organisations, with separate joint councils for each industry. George Hicks advocated as much in his presidential speech to Congress in 1927, although he opposed such moves in 1928, perhaps partly due to his dislike of Mond.[36] It was in this climate that the moves towards the Mond-Turner talks occurred, encouraged by Baldwin, who earlier in the year had pushed for the creation of a new more friendly spirit of industrial relations.

Ultimately, the Mond–Turner talks proved ill-fated but for a couple of years there was an arrangement of types between the trade unions and the employers, particularly in the new and expanding industries. The Mond–Turner negotiations began in November 1928 when Sir Alfred Mond, chairman of ICI, and twenty-one other employers sent a letter to the TUC General Council suggesting 'direct negotiations with the twin objects of the restoration of industrial prosperity and the corresponding improvement in the standard of living of the population'.[37] Although this idea was not universally popular amongst trade unionists it was accepted as being an extension of the joint industrial councils, the Whitley Councils, which had been set up in the early 1920s. Three joint conferences were held between January 1928 and March 1929, three reports were produced covering such issues as trade union recognition, victimisation, industrial relations, unemployment, rationalisation and the gold standard. From these issues, the TUC General Council's main concern was to gain union recognition, from which all the other improvements would emerge.

The employers also hoped for agreements in order to rationalise industry, but matters had not been easy since the Interim Joint Report of the Mond-Turner Conference which advocated rationalisation of industry and co-operation with Labour, was rejected by both the National Conference of Employers' Organisations (NCEO) and the Federation of British Industries (FBI). There was quite clearly a mismatch between the Mond employers, who were mainly in large-scale international industries, based upon science, and the much broader cross-section of British industry represented by the two employers organisations, both of whose members employed around about seven million employees each. These two organisations therefore tended to see a reduction of labour costs as vital to their future

113

rather than the deepening of capital recognised as essential by the employers who supported the Mond initiative. In the end, the Mond–Turner talks failed to establish any particularly close relationships with employers, although they appear to have endorsed the TUC's long-term moves towards industrial conciliation.[38]

If changes occurred in the attitude of trade unions towards the pursuit of industrial muscle they appear to have been incremental rather than revolutionary. Pressures to move in one direction were often countered by moves in the opposite direction, although the overall strategy was evolving gradually. The same could be said about the trade unions and politics. Most trade unionists had distinguished between the industrial and political importance of the General Strike, and the General Council dissociated itself from the latter during the conflict. Even after the strike there was little real evidence that the trade unions had specific political intent, on the rebound from the failure of industrial action. It is true that the General Council took action against the Communist Party of Great Britain and its Minority Movement, but it had already attempted to take such action in 1925 with the nullifying of trades council influence at the TUC Annual conference. In the fullness of time this led to the issuing of the 'Black Circular' of 1934, which demanded the expulsion of Communist delegates from the ranks of the trades councils. Relations with the Labour Party were not so straightforward.

There had been some criticism of Ramsay MacDonald because of his failure to enthuse about the General Strike in 1926. As indicated, he kept himself on the fringes of the dispute, offering his good services in the search for an amicable solution. Essentially, Labour's claim to respectability made the General Strike a great embarrassment. Hence MacDonald was in a difficult position. Nevertheless, one should not ignore the fact that, as in Bradford, in many areas the local secretaries of trades councils were also local secretaries of the Labour parties. The head of the Labour Party might have been as reluctant as Jimmy Thomas to become involved in the dispute but the rank and file, by the very existence of trade-union dominance, were deeply embedded in the struggle. Just about every council of action or trades council that acted in the strike was dominated by Labour Party supporters and activists.

The General Council, of course, greatly strengthened its position within the Labour Party after 1926. There were more trade-union sponsored Labour candidates at the 1929 general election than there had been before but, on the other side of the coin, affiliated trade-union membership of the Labour Party had fallen as a result of the Trades Disputes Act of 1927. Nevertheless, the National Joint Council, later known as the National Council of Labour, formed in 1921 – composed of the National Executive of the Labour Party, the Executive of the Parliamentary Labour Party and the General Council of the TUC – began to be dominated by Ernest Bevin.[39]

Throughout the 1930s, the link between the General Council and the TUC began to develop more closely through the power and influence which Bevin wielded. And one should not ignore the point that Hastings made about Birmingham, where in the wake of the General Strike the support for Labour's political representation increased. In Birmingham, Labour won a parliamentary by-election and increased its representation on the Council from nineteen to thirty-six between 1926 and 1929.[40] Significant developments occurred elsewhere and helped pave the way for Labour's general election victory of May 1929. In addition, the departure of Ramsay MacDonald, Philip Snowden, Jimmy Thomas, and others, in the debacle of 1931 which saw the collapse of the second Labour Government and the formation of a National Government certainly helped to further strengthen the trade union grip on the Labour Party.

Conclusion

It is easy to see the General Strike as a turning point in British industrial relations because of the immensity of the event but the notion simply does not ring true. Although the General Council lost much respect in the immediate wake of defeat it is clear that little of a long-term nature was altered. The trend towards industrial peace continued, albeit through a different format than industrial alliances. It did not make the trade union movement less strike-prone – that was already occurring before 1926 – and it did not make it less determined in its defence of the wages and conditions of the workers, although such a defence took different forms. On balance, Phillips' view seems reasonable and realistic for 'in the end the General Strike merits historical study less for what it changed in the labour movement, than for what it revealed of the unchanging'.[41] On balance more was unchanged than changed.

Notes

1 *Workers' Bulletin*, 13 May 1926. Look at Document Section for how the document continues.

2 Cook, *Nine Days*, p. 23.

3 M. Jacques, 'Consequences of the General Strike', Skelley, *General Strike,*, p. 375.

4 *Ibid.*, p. 377.

5 Bullock, *Bevin*, p. 345.

6 B. Webb, *Diaries, 1924–32*, p. 92, quoted in Bullock, *Bevin*, p. 345.

7 Bullock, *Bevin*, p. 345.

8 *Ibid.*, p. 346.

9 Renshaw, *General Strike*, p. 250.

10 Phillips, *General Strike*; H. A. Clegg, *A History of British Trade Unions since 1889, II, 1911–1933*, Clarendon Press, Oxford, 1985, pp. 383–426; Wrigley, 'Trade Unionists', p. 156.

11 Citrine, *Men and Work*, p. 198.

12 *AEU Monthly Journal*, June 1926.

13 *TUC, Annual Report, 1926*, TUC, London, 1926, p. 70.

14 *Ibid.*, p. 71.

15 *Ibid.*, p. 74.

16 *Ibid.*, pp. 69–76, 388–92.

17 MFGB, *Statement*, pp. 10, 13 and 15.

18 TUC General Council, *Report of Proceedings at a Special Conference of Trade Unions, 20–21 January 1927*, TUC, London, 1927, pp. 4–5, 21–7, 42–3, 45.

19 *Hansard*, 6 March 1925.

20 For the relevant discussions look at Cab 27/327 CP 204 (26), Appendix I; Cab 23/53/33/26, 19 May 1926; Cab 27/327 L (26), 31 May 1926.

21 House of Lords Debates, 4 July 1927.

22 Labour Party Conference, *Annual Report 1939*, Labour Party, London, 1939, p. 92.

23 Labour Party Conference, *Annual Report 1927*, Labour Party, London, 1927, p. 27; TUC, *Annual Report, 1927*, TUC, London, 1927, p. 249.

24 Jacques, 'Consequences of the General Strike', p. 375; J. Foster,'British Imperialism'.

25 Look at Document Section.

26 Jacques, 'Consequences of the General Strike', p. 382.

27 Look at Document Section.

28 W. Citrine, *Manchester Guardian Industrial Relations Supplement*, 30 November 1928, p. 8, quoted in Jacques, 'Consequences of General Strike', p. 386.

29 TUC *Annual Report, 1927*, pp. 316.

30 Jowitt and Laybourn, 'Wool Textile Dispute'.

31 Official unemployment figures rose from 1,243,000 in December 1925 to 1,432,000 in December 1926.

32 G. W. McDonald, 'The Role of British Industry in 1926', in Morris, *General Strike*. Also look at Document Section.

33 TUC, *Annual Report, 1927*, presidential speech.

34 Look at Document Section.

35 Clegg, *British Trade Unions*, p. 421.

36 TUC *Annual Congress Report, 1928*, TUC, London, 1928, pp. 418, 428–9.

37 *Ibid.*, p. 220.

38 See G. W. McDonald and H. F. Gospel, 'The Mond–Turner Talks, 1927–33: A Study in Industrial Co-operation', *Historical Journal*, **xvi**, 4, 1973.

39 Bevin had become a member of the General Council of the TUC in 1925 and was thus automatically a member of the National Joint Council.

40 Hastings, 'Birmingham', p. 272.

41 Phillips, *General Strike*, p. 294.

Conclusion

The General Strike of 1926, the most important conflict in British industrial history, was a product of the economic and social tensions which had been building up in British society in the early 1920s. Although there were many factors which contributed to this conflict it is clear that it was the product of an interplay of circumstances whereby the industrial tensions in the coal industry became inflamed at a time when both the Government and the TUC were moving on a collision course over industrial policies. Whilst governments of the early 1920s were generally geared towards improving industrial relations they harboured the underlying objective of reducing wage levels, and especially so after the return to the Gold Standard and the reflation of the pound in April 1925. A reluctant and conservative TUC also wished to avoid conflict but found that the circumstances of the mining industry and the compelling need to 'expiate the guilt of 1921', when the miners were left without support in their struggle against wage reductions, narrowed its range of options and forced it into a conflict which most of its leading figures – Thomas, Citrine and Bevin – strove to avoid. Indeed, their reluctance to organise support until the last possible moment reflected a view that they could not win and so they drifted into the dispute ill-prepared and with no clear policy or strategy but with the forlorn hope that the miners might accept the compromise arrangements offered by the Samuel Commission.

Once committed to supporting the miners the General Council

had, however reluctantly, to face the fact that its industrial action raised political issues, most obviously the problem that, whether they liked it or not, victory for them would raise the constitutional question of who runs Britain? Baldwin's Conservative Government recognised this, as did the Communist Party, but not the TUC which constantly reiterated its view that it was involved in a national dispute which did not challenge or threaten the Constitution. The General Council fervently believed this to be the case and could not appreciate that its policies were a direct challenge to the Government in so far as they were directed at forcing the Government into taking action to protect the interests of the miners. The General Strike was more than simply sympathetic strike action, more than an alliance between unions directed at the coal owners, it was an attack upon the whole of British society and inevitably challenged the authority of the Baldwin Government. Circumstances beyond their control had pushed the General Council of the TUC in a direction in which it did not want to go and which it knew it could not sustain. In the end, the heart of the trade union movement overruled the reservations of its leaders

The Conservative Government saw the General Strike in constitutional terms and recognised that it could not back away from conflict if it was to maintain any credibility. It prepared for the worst, entertaining the need for significant military involvement but soon scaled down its actions when it realised, after four or five days, that there was no revolutionary intent on the part of the General Council even if the consequences of a trade-union victory might have fundamentally altered the pattern of political control in Britain. It soon realised that its preparations were sufficient and that it was able to control events even if transport, and the railways in particular, had came to an almost complete halt. Nevertheless, given the scale of the dispute there was relatively little violence and the Government was prepared to bide its time and let the trade unions take the decision to retreat in the full knowledge that the Negotiating Committee of the TUC was progressing the Samuel Memorandum in the hope of an end to the dispute. Given that the miners were unlikely to accept it, or the Samuel Report, there was little danger that the Government would be forced to stump up another coal subsidy as it had done in July 1925.

119

E

The Government's faith in the General Council was well founded. The strike was remarkably well organised given the late and haphazard nature of the communications between the General Council, on the one hand, and the trades councils, trade union and the transport committees on the other. Yet in the end the effectiveness of local organisation did not matter for it was a coterie of trade union leaders who decided the outcome. They were aware that their actions would be greeted with outrage. Indeed, Ben Tillett informed Herbert Samuel, on the eve of the termination of the dispute that 'We shall be told we have betrayed the miners. We will get it in the neck, sure.'[1] And, indeed, the General Council was vilified for its actions although the need to maintain some support for the continuing coal dispute led to muted criticism from all but the Communist Party until the beginning of 1927, by which time the threatened legislation against the unions re-inspired a sense of unity within the trade union movement.

Given the scale of the defeat and humiliation of the General Council of the TUC in 1926 it is difficult not to believe that the British trade union movement was damaged by it. Certainly there was some immediate loss of support, its funds were depleted and its leaders under suspicion. None the less, it recovered quickly; the trade union movement does not appear to have been less militant, even if the level of industrial conflict did fall in 1927 and 1928. The fact is that the General Council had been seeking alternatives to industrial conflict well before 1926 and its objective of industrial peace through a unified movement continued, even though it had come to accept the limitations of an industrial alliance after 1926. Thus, it is difficult to view the General Strike as a watershed in British industrial relations.

Nevertheless, the General Strike was an important landmark in the inter-war history of Britain. In many respects it was a lens through which the broader issues of the inter-war years could be viewed. It reflected the problems of declining industries faced with rationalisation and determined that governments would persist with their rationalisation policies. It reflected the tensions which such a policy would produce as a result of the downward pressure on monetary wages. It revealed to the General Council the limits of its own industrial policy, which had been blown up out of proportion by the enormous expansion of trade unions in the First World War and the post-war boom. In the end it revealed that there was to be no compassion by governments, of any political persuasion, for those who faced unemployment and poverty. The fixity of purpose in balancing the budgets of governments, whether under free trade or protection, and the emphasis upon rationalisation ensured that the poor in the declining areas, where the basic industries were struggling, would be neglected. Trade unionism was not weak but it had its limits. And it was fitting that when the trade union movement had the opportunity to put the record straight it did so. In 1946, in abolishing the 1927 Trades Disputes Act, Bevin told the House of Commons that:

> I propose this afternoon to deal with the historical side of the General Strike. I have been waiting twenty years to do this. They cast the trade unions as the enemies of the State . . . (but) this was not a strike against the state. It was a strike in support of people whose wages were at the lowest possible level . . . and from which certain powers . . . sought unjustly to drive them lower . . . (by a) miserable attack on the standard of life of men in a basic industry.[2]

Notes

1 Citrine, *Men and Work*, p. 198.
2 *Hansard*, 12 February 1946.

121

Selected documents

Document 1

Emergency Powers Act, 1920
10 & 11 Geo. V., ch. 55.

(1) If at any time it appears to his Majesty that there have occurred, or are about to occur, events of such a nature as to be calculated by interfering with the supply and distribution of food, water, fuel, or light, or with the means of locomotion, to deprive the community, or any substantial portion of the community, of the essentials of life, His Majesty may, by proclamation (hereinafter referred to as a proclamation of emergency), declare that a state of emergency exists.

Document 2

The formation of the General Council of the TUC, 1921
The General Council of the Trades Union Congress: its Powers, Functions, and Work, TUC, London, 1925.

The advent of the General Council marks a very great stride forward in the direction of a Labour General Staff. That idea has not yet been realised. In the view of many trade unionists, it will not be achieved until Trades Unions assent to the creation of a controlling body sitting in continuous session and devoting its whole time to the tasks of organisation, the co-ordination of effort, and the planning of industrial action on scientific lines.

Document 3

Red Friday, 31 July 1925.
Labour Magazine, August 1925 and W. Citrine, *Men and Work*,
Hutchinson, London, 1964, p. 174.

> In my opinion it would be mistaken to overrate the apparent
> success which attended the General Council's efforts in support of
> the miners, and later the textile workers, in their struggle to
> maintain essential Trade Union principles. . . . I was convinced
> that in limiting the scope of the action which it was proposed to
> take in the mining dispute and in basing our strategy upon the
> transport and railway unions – which incidentally cannot always
> be expected to act as the storm troops of the movement – the
> General Council acted wisely. Had it been necessary to call a
> general stoppage we should have realised where our weakness
> lay.
> Responsibility for calling a strike and for organising the neces-
> sary financial and other measures is not concentrated in the
> General Council to such an extent that many – perhaps the
> majority – even of trade union executives could not constitu-
> tionally act without the sanction of a ballot vote of their members.

Document 4

The Wool Textile Workers' and Miners disputes of 1925
Yorkshire Factory Times, 27 August 1925.

> General Council's action in support of the miners and wool textile
> workers signalised a turn in the tide, the beginning of a definite
> stand against the policy of wage reductions which economic con-
> ditions have enabled the employers to impose in the last four and a
> half years.

Document 5

The Organisation for the Maintenance of Supplies
Quoted in R. P. Arnot, *The Miners: Years of Struggle: A History of the
Miners' Federation of Great Britain (from 1910 onwards*, Allen &
Unwin, London, 1953, p. 393.

> For many months past it has been evident that a movement is
> being organised to take advantage of a trade dispute, exceptionally
> difficult to solve, in order to promote a general strike. Numerous

suggestions have since been made from various quarters for organising those citizens who would be prepared to volunteer to maintain supplies and vital services in the event of a general strike.

It seems, therefore, that the movement has come to announce publicly that such an organisation has already been constituted and is at work in many metropolitan boroughs, while steps are being taken to create corresponding organisations in all principal centres in the kingdom.

Document 6

Industrial disputes: the powers of the General Council
TUC, *Report*, 1926, pp. 91–3, reporting upon resolutions and amendments put to the Scarborough Conference of September 1925 and subsequent discussions.

COMPOSITE RESOLUTION

That this Trade Union Congress is of the opinion that the time is now ripe for definite powers to be given to the General Council, as follows:

1. To have power to levy all affiliated members.

2. To call for a stoppage of work by an affiliated organisation, or part thereof, in order to assist a union defending a vital Trade Union principle, and also have powers to arrange with the C.W.S. to make provision for the distribution of food, etc., in the event of a strike or other action calling for same.

3. That this Congress calls on all organisations to make such alteration to rules to regularise the above position.

AMENDMENTS

Amendment to Clause 1: Delete the words 'To have power to levy all affiliated members.'

Amendment: 'That this Congress while welcoming all efforts to co-ordinate the aims of the Movement generally with a view to securing the greatest possible economic results for the workers as a whole, deprecate any proposals having for their object the interfering with the right of affiliated societies to secure alteration of their working conditions or the substituting of the principle of the general strike in place of the present method of each industry proceeding in the way best suited to its own needs and possibilities.'

On the instructions of Congress the whole subject was referred to the General Council to examine the problem in all its bearings, with power to consult the Executive of the affiliated Unions and to report to a special conference of the Executives concerned their considered recommendations on the subject.

This resolution was considered fully by the General Council who, in a circular dated 4th February, 1926, explained to the affiliated Unions that they did not feel it necessary to call a special conference on Executives on the specific subject.

In considering the matter, the Council had regard to the fact that in respect of the suggested power to levy affiliated societies, as expressed in Clause 1 of the composite resolution, a similar proposition had been rejected twice by recent Congresses, namely, the Southport Congress, 1922, and the Plymouth Congress, 1923.

Subsequent to these Congresses, the General Council were given additional powers under Standing Order No. 11, clause (d) of which gives the Council power to organise all such moral and material support on behalf of a union in dispute with employers, as the circumstances of the dispute appear to justify . . . Clause 2 of the composite resolution would give the Council power to order a stoppage of work by any affiliated organisations or any number of the members of such organisations, in order to assist a union defending a vital Trade Union principle.

The Council in considering this point felt that great difficulties would be experienced in obtaining such a mandate from the unions. It would necessitate very drastic alterations of the constitutions of many unions, and the Council considered that unions were not likely to surrender such a measure of autonomy until they had had greater experience of the manner in which the Council were able to utilise the recent powers entrusted to them. . . .

The National Strike has since proved that there is no lack of readiness on the part of affiliated unions to respond to such an appeal for assistance where it is felt that some vital principle affecting the Movement as a whole is imperilled.

Document 7

Constitution of Industrial Alliance, November, 1925.
R. P. Arnot, *The General Strike, May 1926: Its Origins*, Labour Research Department, 1926, pp. 83–6. This is a small part of the constitution of an ill-fated attempt by the miners to organise an industrial alliance with other unions in transport and heavy industry.

1. *Objects*
To create through a Trade Union Alliance a means of mutual

support and to admit any or all of the allied organisations:

(a) To defend hours of labour and wages standards.

(b) To promote or defend any vital principle of an industrial character.

To take such steps for mutual co-operation on economic and industrial matters as may from time to time be decided upon.

2. *Constitution*
The Alliance shall consist of organisations representing work-people engaged in all forms of transport (Railway, Docks, Waterways, Road, Sea, Air), Engineering, Shipbuilding, Iron and Steel production, Mining and all forms of Power production and Distribution.

3. *Government of the Alliance (General Conference)*
For the government of the Alliance there shall be a General Conference. Those eligible to attend must be either officers and/or members of the Executive Council of allied organisation. Such Conference shall meet at least once per year in London; also at such times as may be called by the Executive Council hereinafter provided.

Document 8

Statement of the Executive Committee of the Communist Party of Great Britain
Workers' Weekly, 15 January 1926.

The present industrial situation and crisis looming ahead fully justified the Communist Party's warning to the workers that the Capitalist class is determined to return to the offensive, on an even more gigantic scale than last July.

The miners, after breathing space bought from the owners by means of a subsidy, and the sham impartiality of the Coal Commission, are now threatened with an open attack on the seven-hour day, on the Miners' Federation and on wages.

The attack upon the miners is the most violent and unashamed; but workers in most of the industries are faced with similar attacks.

The railwaymen are threatened with wage cuts; the engineers with longer hours: the builders with the abolition of craft control won by years of sacrifice. . . .

These facts taken together with the steady, if unobtrusive organisation of the OMS [Organisation for Maintenance of

Supplies], point to a definite determination on the part of British capitalists to prevent a repetition of Red Friday, to challenge the organised Labour movement and to smash it, and to drive the workers down to coolie conditions. . . .

The struggle now opening is of a magnitude hitherto unknown. But this enlarged meeting of the Central Committee of the Communist Party believes that the workers can meet the capitalist attack and smash it, as on Friday.

Document 9

Report of the Royal Commission on the Coal Industry (the Samuel Commission), 1925–6
Report of the Royal Commission on the Coal Industry (1925), I: Report, Cmd 2600, pp. 235–7.

The dominant fact is that, in the last quarter of 1925, if the subsidy be excluded, 73 per cent of the coal was produced at a loss.

We express no opinion whether the grant of a subsidy last July was unavoidable or not, but we think its continuance indefensible. The subsidy should stop at the end of its authorised term, and should never be repeated.

We cannot approve the proposal of the Mining Association, that the gap between costs and proceeds should be bridged by an increase of an hour in the working day, reduction in miners' wages, some economics in other costs, and a large diminution in railway rates to be effected by lowering the wages of railwaymen. In any case these proposals go beyond the need, for we do not concur in the low estimates of coal prices on which they are based.

. . . If the present hours are to be retained, we think a revision of the 'minimum percentage addition to the standard rate of wages', fixed in 1924 at a time of temporary prosperity, is indispensable. . . . The reductions that we contemplate will still leave the mine-owners without adequate profits in any of the wage-agreement districts. . . .

Should the miners freely prefer some extension of hours with less reduction of wages, Parliament would no doubt be prepared to authorise it. We trust, however, that this will not occur.

Conclusion

. . . The way to prosperity for the mining industry lies along three chief lines of advance: through greater application of science to the winning and using of coal, through larger units of production and distribution, through fuller partnership between employers and employed. In all three respects progress must come mainly from within the industry. The State can help materially – by substantial payments in aid of research; by removing obstacles to amalgamation under existing leases; as owner of the minerals by determining the condition of new leases; by legislation for the establishment of pit committees and of profit-sharing, and in other ways.

Document 10

General Council of TUC 'proposal for co-ordinated action, put to the trade unions on 30 April 1926 and adopted 1 May' (TUC General Council, *The Mining Crisis and the National Strike*, TUC, London, June 1926, pp. 32A).

1. *Scope*
The Trades Union Congress General Council and the Miners' Federation of Great Britain having been unable to obtain a satisfactory settlement of the matters in dispute in the coalmining industry, and the Government and the mineowners having forced a lockout, the General Council, in view of the need for co-ordinated action on the part of the affiliated unions in defence of the policy laid down by the General Council of the Trades Union Congress, directs as follows:
TRADES AND UNDERTAKINGS TO CEASE WORK
Except as hereinafter provided, the following trades and undertakings shall cease work as and when required by the General Council:
Transport, including all affiliated unions connected with Transport i.e. railways, sea transport. . . .
Printing trades, including the Press.
Productive industries. (a) Iron and steel. (b) Metal and Heavy Chemical Group. Including all metal workers and other workers who are engaged, or may be engaged, in installing alternative plant to take the place of coal.
Building trade. All workers engaged on building, except such as are employed definitely in housing and hospital work . . . shall cease work.
Electricity and gas. . . . Trade Unions connected with the supply of electricity and gas shall co-operate with the object of ceasing to

supply power. The Council request that the Executives of the Trade Unions concerned shall meet at once with a view to formulating common policy.

Sanitary services. The General Council direct that sanitary services be continued.

Health and food services. The General Council recommend that there should be no interference in regard to these, and that the Trade Union concerned should do everything in their power to organise the distribution of milk and food to the whole population.

With regard to hospitals, clinics, convalescent homes, sanatoria, infant welfare centres, maternity homes, nursing homes, schools, the General Council direct that every affiliated union take every opportunity to ensure that food, milk, medical and surgical supplies shall be efficiently provided.

2. Trade Union discipline.

. . . (b) The General Council recommend that the actual calling out of the workers should be left to the unions, and instructions should only be issued by the accredited representatives of the unions participating in the dispute.

3. Trades Councils

The work of the Trades Councils, in conjunction with the local officers of the trade unions actually participating in the dispute, shall be to assist in carrying out the foregoing provisions (i.e. stoppage of work in various trades and undertakings, and the exceptions thereto), and they shall be charged with the responsibility of organising the trade unionists in dispute in the most effective manner for the preservation of peace and order . . .

. . .

6. Procedure

(a) These proposals shall be immediately considered by the Executive of the Trade Unions concerned in the stoppage, who will at once report as to whether they will place their powers in the hands of the General Council and carry out the instructions which the General Council may issue from time to time concerning the necessary action and conduct of the dispute.

(b) And, further, that the Executives of all other affiliated unions are asked to report at once as to whether they will place their powers in the hands of the General Council and carry out the instructions of the General Council from time to time, both regarding the conduct of the dispute and financial assistance.

A. Pugh, Chairman

Walter M. Citrine, Acting Secretary.

129

Document 11

Government announcement of the impending strike, 3 May 1926
Quoted in the *Leeds Mercury, 3 May 1926.*

His Majesty's Government believes that no solution of the difficulties of the coal industry, which is both practical and honourable to all concerned, can be reached except by sincere acceptance of the report of the Commission.

In the expression 'acceptance of the report' is included both the re-organisation of the industry which should be put in hand immediately and pending the realisation and re-organisation of the industry being attained, an interim adjustment of wages, or hours of work, as will make it economically possible to carry on the industry.

In the meantime, if the miners or the T.U.C. on their behalf, were prepared to say plainly they accepted the proposal, the Government would have been ready to resume the negotiations and to continue the subsidy for a fortnight; but since the discussion which has taken place between the Ministers and the members of the T.U.C. it has come to the knowledge of the Government, not only that specific instructions have been sent – under the authority of the Executive of Trade Union representatives at the Conference convened by the General Council of the Trades Union Congress – directing their members in several of the most vital industries and services of the country to carry out a strike on Tuesday next, but that overt acts have already taken place including gross interference with the freedom of the Press.

Such action involves the challenge to the constitutional right and freedom of the nation.

His Majesty's Government, therefore, before they can continue negotiations, must require from the Trade Union Committee both the repudiation of the actions referred to as having already taken place, and the immediate and unconditional withdrawal of the instructions for a general strike.

Document 12

Winston Churchill MP on the issue of trade unions helping to move supplies of food
Hansard, 3 May 1926, col. 123.

I readily recognise the offer which was made to convey food and necessaries by the Trade Union Committee. . . . It may have been a wise thing for the trade unions to have done, but, . . . what Government in the World could enter into partnership with a rival Government, against which it is endeavouring to defend itself and society, and allow that rival Government to sit in judgement on every train that runs and on every lorry on the road.

Document 13

Councillor W. Mellor, secretary of Manchester Trades and Labour Council on Food distribution
Times, 4 May 1926.

I anticipate that we shall act as the food distributors under the voluntary system agreed upon by the trade unions, *but we have no definite instructions to point to yet*. It may be that the railway workers and the transport workers will carry out the distribution under their own direction.

Document 14

Ministry of Health circular 703, 5 May 1926

> Circular 703
> MINISTRY OF HEALTH,
> Whitehall, S.W. I,
> 5th May, 1926

Board of Guardians
 (England and Wales).

Sir,
I am directed by the Ministry of Health to transmit for the consideration of the Guardians the following notes and suggestions with reference to the action to be taken in view of the general stoppage of industry.

It is to be anticipated that there may be large numbers of applications for relief arising directly or indirectly out of the stoppage, and it will be necessary on the one hand for the Guardians to make adequate arrangements for carrying out their statutory duty of relieving destitution and on the other to take all possible steps to conserve their financial resources in face of the demands that may be made upon them, and the possibly prolonged duration of the stoppage. An emergency like the present makes it the plain duty of every Board to keep this second consideration always before them in deciding what they can properly do.

131

. . . The function of the Guardians is the relief of destitution within the limits prescribed by law and they are in no way concerned in the merits of an industrial dispute, even though it results in application for relief. They cannot, therefore, properly give any weight to their views of such merits in dealing with the application to be made.

The questions for consideration of the Guardians on any application for relief made by the person who is destitute in consequence of a trade dispute are questions of fact, namely, whether the applicant for relief is or is not a person who is able-bodied and physically capable of work; whether work is or is not available for him and if such work is not available for him, whether it is or not so unavailable through his own act or consent.

Where the applicant for relief is able-bodied and physically capable of work the grant of relief to him is unlawful if work is available for him or he is thrown on the Guardians through his own act or consent. . .

Document 15

TUC General Announcement, 7 May 1926
Leeds Mercury, 8 May 1926.

Local strike organisations are authorised to offer to meet employers immediately and to offer to supply light and power for such services as house, street and shop lighting, social services and power for food, bakeries, laundries and domestic purposes.

'Will you therefore approach local undertakings and report their reply?'

Mr. E. L. Phillips, Chairman of the General Council, pointed out that the present struggle was industrial and not political. The General Council, he emphasised, did not challenge the Constitution, and were not seeking to substitute an unconstitutional Government or to undermine the Constitution.

They were endeavouring to secure better conditions of living for the miners. They were struggling hard, and were anxious for an honourable peace as soon as possible. If negotiations were to be resumed their desire was to enter into these unfettered.

Document 16

Sir John Simon on the illegality of the General Strike
Hansard, 6 May 1926.

By referring to it as a 'general strike' there has grown in some quarters a belief that this situation is the same in character as previous strikes, though of course on a vastly greater scale. This was not the case and the strike was an attempt to coerce the Government.

Every workman who was bound by a contract to give notice before he left work, and who . . . has either chosen of his own free will or has felt compelled to come out by leaving his employment without proper notice, has broken the law.

Document 17

The Prime Minister, Stanley Baldwin, broadcasts on the BBC, Saturday, 8 May 1926
Reported in the *Leeds Mercury*, 10 May 1926.

What is the issue for which the Government is fighting? It is fighting because while negotiations were still in progress the T.U.C. ordered a general strike, presumably to force Parliament and the community to heed its will.

With that object the T.U.C. has declared that the railways shall not run, that transport shall not move and that the unloading of ships shall stop, and that no news shall reach the public. The supply of electricity, the transportation of food supplies of the people have been interrupted.

The T.U.C. declare that this is merely an industrial dispute, but their method of helping the miners is to affect the community.

Can there be a more direct attack upon the community than that a body not elected by the voters of the country, without consulting even trade unionists, and in order to impose conditions never yet defined should disrupt the life of the nation and try to starve it into submission?

I wish to make it as clear as I can that the Government is not fighting to lower the standard of living of the miners or of any other class of workers.

My whole desire is to maintain the standard of living of every worker, and I am ready to press the employers to make every sacrifice to this end, consistent with keeping industry in its proper working order.

This is the Government's position. The general strike must be called off absolutely and without reserve. The mining dispute can then be settled. . . .

I am a man of peace. I am longing and working and praying for peace. But I will not surrender the safety and security of the British Constitution.

You placed me in power eighteen months ago by the largest majority afforded to any party for many years.

Have I done anything to forfeit that confidence? Cannot you trust me to ensure a square deal for the parties and secure even justice between man and man?

Document 18

The TUC: Where We Stand, 10 May 1926
British Worker, Manchester edition, 10 May 1926.

WHERE WE STAND

It is being persistently stated that Mr. Ramsay MacDonald, Mr. Herbert Samuel, Mr. Arthur Cook and other Trade Union leaders have been engaged in an attempt to re-open negotiations with a view to ending the General Stoppage.

The General Council wish it to be clearly understood that there is no truth in this assertion.

No official or unofficial overtures have been made to the Government by any individual or group of individuals, either with or without the sanction of the General Council. Complete control of all negotiations is vested in the General Council, who have had no direct or indirect communication with the Government since they sent their emphatic letter of protest against the Cabinet's wanton action in wrecking the peace discussions that were proceeding.

The position of the General Council may be stated in simple and unequivocal terms. They are ready at a moment to enter into preliminary discussions regarding the withdrawal of the lock-out notices and ending in the General Stoppages and the resumption of negotiations for an honourable settlement of the Mining Dispute. These preliminary discussions must be free from any condition.

The Government must remember, and the public are asked to remember, that the General Stoppage took place as a result of the action of the Cabinet in breaking off peace discussions and issuing their ultimatum, using as their excuse the unauthorised action of the printing staff of a London newspaper. The responsibility of the present grave situation rests entirely upon the Cabinet. Even the newspapers concerned admit it to be true 'that when the negotiations broke down the trade union representatives knew nothing of the stopping of "The Daily Mail".'

It is therefore merely fantastic for the Prime Minister to pretend that the Trade Unions are engaged in an attack upon the Constitution of the Country. Every instruction issued by the General Council is evidence of their determination to maintain the struggle strictly on the basis of an industrial dispute. They have ordered every member taking part to be exemplary in his conduct and not to give any cause for police interference.

The General Council struggled hard for peace. They are anxious that an honourable peace shall be secured as soon as possible.

They are not attacking the Constitution. They are fighting the community. They are defending the mine workers against the mine owners.

Document 19

TUC Reply to Mr. Baldwin
British Worker, 11 May 1926.

Our Reply to Mr. Baldwin's Broadcast
The workers must not be misled by Mr. Baldwin's renewed attempt last night to represent the present strike as a political issue. The trade unions are fighting for one thing, and one thing only, to protect the miners' standard of life.

The General Council never broke off negotiations. This was done by the Cabinet upon an isolated and unauthorised incident at a most promising stage of discussion.

The General Council is prepared at any moment to resume those negotiations where they had left off. It has been urged to do so by the united churches of the country, led by the Archbishop of Canterbury. But his appeal was withheld from the nation by the Broadcasting Company. Why?

The Prime Minister pleads for justice. He can get justice by going back to the Friday before the mineworkers' lock-out notices took effect and recreating the atmosphere of hope which prevailed. . . .

The General Council has never closed any door that might be kept open for negotiation. It has done nothing to imperil the food supplies; on the contrary, its members were instructed to co-operate with the Government in maintaining them. No notice has been taken of this offer.

The Prime Minister pleads for peace, but insists that the General Council is challenging the Constitution. This is untrue.
The General Council does not challenge one rule, law or custom of the Constitution; it asks only that the miners be safeguarded. . . .

The General Council does NOT challenge the Constitution. It is not seeking to substitute unconstitutional government. Nor is it

F

desirous of undermining our Parliamentary Institutions.

The sole aim of the Council is to secure for the Miners a decent standard of living.

The Council is engaged in an Industrial dispute.

In any settlement, the only issue to be decided will be an industrial issue, not political, not constitutional.

There is no Constitutional Crisis.

Document 20

The Samuel Memorandum and correspondence relating to it
TUC Archives and in several local collections.

a. A. Pugh.,
President, General Council,
Trades Union Congress.   May 12th, 1926

Dear Mr. Pugh,

At the outcome of the conversations which I have had with your Committee, I attach a memorandum enbodying the conclusions that have been reached.

I have made it clear to your Committee from the outset that I have been acting entirely on my own initiative, have received no authority from the Government, and can give no assurance on their behalf.

I am of opinion that the proposals embodied in the Memorandum are suitable for adoption and are likely to promote a settlement of the differences in the Coal Industry.

I shall strongly recommend their acceptance by the Government when the negotiations are renewed.

Yours sincerely.

(Signed) HERBERT SAMUEL

b. Sir Herbert Samuel,
London.   12 May 1926

Dear Sir,

The General Council having carefully considered your letter of to-day and the memorandum attached to it, concurred in your opinion that it offers a basis on which the negotiations upon the conditions in the Coal Industry can be renewed.

They are taking the necessary measures to terminate the General Strike, relying upon public assurances of the Prime Minister as to the steps that would follow. They assume that during the resumed negotiations the subsidy will be renewed and that the lockout notices to the Miners will be immediately withdrawn.

Yours faithfully,

(Signed) ARTHUR PUGH, Chairman

WALTER CITRINE, Acting Secretary

c. Memorandum

1. The negotiations upon the conditions of the coal industry should be resumed, the subsidy being renewed for such reasonable period as may be required for that purpose.

2. Any negotiations are unlikely to be successful unless they provide for means of settling disputes in the industry other than conferences between the mine-owners and they alone. A National Wages board should, therefore, be established which would include representatives of the two parties with a neutral element and an independent Chairman. The proposals in this direction tentatively made in the Report of the Royal Commission should be pressed and the powers of the proposed Board enlarged.

3. The parties of the Board should be entitled to raise before it any points they consider relevant to the issues under discussion.

4. There should be no revision of the previous wage rates unless there are sufficient assurances that the measures of reorganisation proposed by the Commission will be effectively adopted. A Committee should be established as proposed by the Prime Minister on which representatives of the men should be included, whose duty it should be to co-operate with the Government in the preparation of the legislative and administrative measures that are required. The same Committee, or alternatively, the National Wages Board, should assure itself that the necessary steps, so far as they relate to matters within the industry, are not being neglected or unduly postponed.

5. After these points have been agreed and the Mines National Wages Board has considered every practicable means of meeting such immediate financial difficulties as exist, it may, if that course is found to be absolutely necessary, proceed to the preparation of a wage agreement.

6. Any such agreement should

   (i) if practicable, be on simpler lines than those hitherto followed.

   (ii) not adversely affect in any way the wages of the lowest paid men.

   (iii) fix reasonable figures below which the wage of no class of

137

labour, for a normal customary week's work, should be reduced in any circumstance.

(iv) in the event if any new adjustments being made, should provide for the revision of such adjustments by the Wages Board from time to time if facts warrant that course.

7. Measures should be adopted to prevent the recruitment of new workers, over the age of 18 years, into the industry if unemployed miners are available.

8. Workers who are displaced as a consequence of the closing of uneconomic collieries should be provided for by

(a) The transfer of such men as may be mobile, with the Government assistance that may be required, as recommended in the Report of the Royal Commission.

(b) The maintenance, for such period as may be fixed, of those who cannot be transferred, and for whom alternative employment cannot be found, this maintenance to compose in addition to the existing rate of unemployment paid under the Unemployment Insurance Act, of such amount as may be agreed. A contribution should be made by treasury to cover the additional sums so disbursed.

(c) The rapid construction of new houses to accommodate transferred workers. The Trades Union Congress will facilitate this by consultation and co-operation with all those who are concerned.

Document 21

The TUC calls off the General Strike
TUC Archives and some local collections contain the following circular.

TO THE SECRETARIES OF AFFILIATED TRADE UNIONS AND FOR THE INFORMATION OF TRADES COUNCILS AND STRIKE COMMITTEES.
Dear Sir or Madam.

The General Council, through the magnificent support and solidarity of the Trade Union Movement has obtained assurances that a settlement of the Mining problem can be secured which justifies them in bringing the general stoppage to an end.

Conversations have been proceeding between the General Council representatives and Sir Herbert Samuel, Chairman of the Coal Commission, who returned from Italy for the express purpose of offering his services to try to effect a settlement of the differences in the Coal Mining Industry.

138

The Government has declared that under no circumstances could negotiations take place until the general strike had been terminated, but the General Council feel as a result of the conversations with Sir Herbert Samuel and the proposals which are embodied in the correspondence and documents which are enclosed that sufficient assurances had been obtained as to the lines upon which a settlement could be reached to justify them in terminating the General Strike.

The General Council accordingly decided at their meeting to-day to terminate the general stoppage, in order that negotiations could be resumed to secure a settlement in the coal mining industry, free and unfettered from either strike or lock-out.

The General Council considered the practicability of securing resumption of work by the members in dispute at uniform time and date, but it was felt, having regard to the varied circumstances and practice in each industry, that it would be better for each Executive Council itself to make arrangements for the resumption of work of its own members. The following telegram was dispatched to you to-day:

General Council TUC have today declared General Strike terminated. Please instruct your members as to resuming work as soon as arrangements can be made. Letter follows.

Pugh. Citrine

. . .

The General Council accept the consequences of their decision with a full sense of their responsibility not only to their own membership but to the Nation at large. They have endeavoured throughout the crisis to conduct their case as industrial disputes have always been conducted by British Trade Unions, without violence or aggression. The General Council feel in taking the last steps to bring the crisis to an end that the Trade Union Movement has given a demonstration to the World of discipline, unity and loyalty without parallel in the history of industrial disputes.

Yours fraternally,

ARTHUR PUGH, Chairman

WALTER M. CITRINE, Acting Secretary

Document 22

Stanley Baldwin, Prime Minister, to the House of Commons, 12 May 1926
Hansard, 12 May 1926.

The President of the Trade Union Council this morning came, and told me, that they have decided to call off the general strike forthwith. I said that it would be the immediate effort of myself and my colleagues to bring about a resumption of negotiations between the two parties in the mining industry with a view to securing the earliest possible settlement. I will only add this – the peace which has come at this moment is a victory for the common sense of the whole of the people of the United Kingdom. It is of the utmost importance at a moment like this that the British people should not look backwards but forward.

We should resume our work in a spirit of co-operation and put behind us all malice and vindictiveness.

Document 23

Report of the Liverpool Council of Action
Copies in possession of Keith Laybourn and also in General Strike Collection, 333 TRA 4, Liverpool Archives.

In submitting this report from the Liverpool Trades Council and Labour Party we realised some twelve months ago that trouble lay ahead in connection with the Mining Industry, and therefore we decided to take what, in our opinion, seemed to be necessary steps for bringing about co-ordination and unification amongst the Trade Union Organisations within the Merseyside areas, and therefore we brought into being a 'Provisional Council of Action'.

Invitations were therefore extended to Trade Union Organisations and Federations in August last, and the first meeting of the 'Provisional Council' was held on Wednesday evening March 24th 1926. At that meeting representatives were present from all the Trade Union Federations within the Merseyside area. At that meeting a provisional Chairman and Secretary were elected, and the meeting dispersed with an instruction that the Chairman and the Secretary should convene the next meeting as soon as information and instructions were received from the TUC.

In view of the developments that took place, the members of the 'Provisional Council of Action' were called together for Sunday 2nd May, and at that meeting it was decided that the 'Provisional Committee' should become the 'Council of Action' for the area comprising Liverpool, Bootle, Birkenhead and Wallasey.

The Organisations represented upon the Council were as follows: Transport & General Workers' Union, Carters' and Motormens' Union, Enginemen and Shipbuilding Federation, Building

Trades Federation, Building Trade Workers, A.E.U., Printing and Kindred Trades Federation, N.U.R., A.S.L.E.F., R.C.A., National Union of Distributive and Allied Workers, Shipwrights, Boilermakers', Liverpool Trades Council, Birkenhead Trades Council, Bootle Trades Council and Wallasay Trades Council. The three Merseyside Members of Parliament, Messrs Hayes, Gibbins and Secton, were later co-opted members of the 'Council of Action'.

The Council of Action were in continual session from the beginning of the General Strike until its termination, and grouped round them were the respective Strike Committees connected with the following Industries: Transport Trades, Building Trades, Distributive Trades etc., who maintained contact with the 'Council of Action' by the appointment of liaison officers.

A Publicity Committee was set up consisting of five representatives and during the period of the strike 500,000 bulletins were issued and circulated throughout the whole of the Merseyside area. This was only possible by mobilising from the respective Trade Union officers, duplicating machines, of which 14 were placed at our disposal.

Arrangements were also made for the holding of meetings etc., and during the period of stoppage 72 meetings were held in the Merseyside area which were attended by thousands of people. In many cases where halls were booked, huge overflow meetings had to be held in the open space in the vicinity.

Viewing the position from the Merseyside point of view the response made by the workers to the General Council's appeal was magnificent. The greatest difficulty we had to face during the Strike, was the lack of definite instructions and contact with the Trades Union Congress General Council. Any instructions we received were indirect, i.e. from the Trades Union Organisations attached to the Council of Action. This in my opinion was a weakness, all instructions should have been sent from the T.U.C. to the 'Local Council of Action' and the responsibility of carrying out the same should have been theirs.

(Signed) W. H. Barton.

Document 24

Extracts from the questionnaire circulated by the Labour Research Department and sent to the Trades Council towards the end of 1926
E. Burns, *The General Strike (May, 1926): Trades Councils in Action*,

141

Labour Research Department, London, 1926, pp. 104–5, 112–15, 123, 131, 134–5, 159.

Bolton

Organisation – Wired to all E. C. members of the Local Trades Council as Emergency Committee. Decided to form a Central Committee under the title of the 'Bolton Council of Action'. Committee composed of the Secretary of every local Union affected directly or indirectly by the General Strike. Other secretaries were brought in as soon as they were affected. President of the Trades Council appointed Chairman and Secretary along with self. I am Labour Agent in Bolton and, as a full-time Agent with an Office, telephone, and Gestetner Rotary machine, was also appointed Joint Secretary. We formed the following Sub-Committees – Office, Staff, Organisation, Transport, Publicity, Finance, Public Committees, Picketing, Vital Services, Messengers. All Railway Unions had, in addition, a Strike Committee, and a representative was on the above Council. All their efforts were co-ordinated by us, and the Council was the sole authoritative body all through, taking our instructions from the North Western Area Council, who in turn received theirs from the T.U.C. General Council. The Council of Action is retained in the meantime to assist in the direction of helping the Miners by a Relief Fund and feeding of Miners' kiddies; and helping where possible to secure the return to work of victimised strikers. Future of the Council to be finally determined.

Arrangements with Co-op – No arrangements whatever were made with the Co-operative Society. It is largely a Conservative body, and non-sympathetic. They did not offer to help us in any way at all.

Special points . . . Powerful wireless set installed the first day of the strike. 2280 pickets mobilised in two days. Every picket did four hours on and twenty hours off. All were badged with a white silk ribbon. 29 push bikes and 57 motor bikes mobilised for picket and messenger work. Two local Cinemas granted free use of Cinemas in morning and afternoon meeting of strikers. Contact originated and maintained with practically every town in Lancashire each day. From Lancaster to Todmorden and from Macclesfield to Liverpool. No open-air meetings held at all. We kept our people off the streets as far as possible . . .

Publicity – We ran a bulletin every day, commencing on Saturday,

May 8, 1926, when we published morning, noon and evening. Published from Saturday, May 8, 1926, to Saturday, May 15, 1926, inclusive. 4000 to 5000 copies daily, a total of 38,000 copies – free. Not likely to be continued, as the Bolton Labour Press run a *Bolton Labour News* in similar form, which will serve local purposes.

Arrests In Bolton proper, none. . . .
Coventry
Organisation [Preparations for an engineering dispute.] A Council of Action of 50 was thus rapidly formed; it did not become unwieldy, and proved a very live body. It is hoped that the Council of Action will continue to function as a trade union organising committee.

Arrangements with Co-op – No definite arrangements were made with the Co-op, but it did play a prominent part in the struggle. It placed a car at the disposal of the Council of Action, and also gave facilities in the way of duplicating 'Speakers' Notes,' supplied copies of verbatim wireless reports. . . . On the other hand, the Co-op used the Council of Action in securing permits for the release of food supplies, and also in securing for them permission from the Warwickshire Miners' Association to obtain a supply of coal for domestic purposes from one of the local pits. The Co-op also played an important part in controlling prices. At a meeting of tradesmen and Trades Council representatives on Monday, 3rd May, convened by the local Food Controller, the chairman of the Co-op intimated that for at least 14 days there would be no increase. The local vultures were obviously bitterly disappointed. . . .

Special points – . . . In the first place, the response to the dispute was magnificent; . . . A Transport Committee controlled all transport for despatch riding, etc. . . . In addition, Coventry was made a centre by the General Council for the distribution of propaganda, etc., to Rugby, Warwick, Leamington, Nuneaton, Hinckley, and Bedworth. . . .

Publicity – The Publicity Committee issued a number of Strike Bulletins, but here there certainly appears to have been a weakness, inasmuch as adequate copies do not appear to have been filed. Where a supply of *British Workers* were expected in the morning, a bulletin would be issued in the evening and vice versa. About 200 of each issue were duplicated. It will not be continued,

143

because a *Labour Monthly* was already being published before the strike.

Dorking and District

Organisation – The N.U.R. being the largest unit, acted separately as a Strike Committee.

Special points – Bad; the ignoring of the Trades Council. No arrangements with the Co-op. No local bulletins issued.

Arrests None.

Position on 12 May – A little weakening.

Hendon

Organisation Trades Council only just formed and strike run by a Joint Strike Committee, representatives of all unions involved. Not yet disbanded, but not likely to remain in existence as Trades Council should be functioning.

Publicity – Bulletin run for five days – May 7 to 12th. About 60 copies each issue. Now starting a four-page monthly.

Arrests – Two.

Leeds

Organisation – Trades Council Executive and Council of Action acted as one committee. Officials and representatives of unions concerned acted separately as another committee, but a number of people sat on both. Committees are still in existence, but really nothing is doing, apart from raising funds to help distressed and victimised workers.

Arrangements with Co-op – None.

Special points – Nothing particular. One responsible Strike Committee would have been preferable.

Publicity – We normally produce a local weekly. During the strike a typed bulletin was issued, average about 1000 daily. A printed bulletin was issued two days – 5,000 and 12,000 respectively; and the *British Worker* one day (last day of the strike), circulation about 7,000. Continued as before the strike as our local Labour weekly – *Leeds Weekly Citizen*.

Arrests – Cannot say definitely, but about 10 or 12, nothing serious.

Perth

Organisation – Strike Committee. This is being retained as an organising Committee – one member for each Union affiliated.

Arrangements with Co-op – Most of the Unions were accommodated by local Society for money whilst waiting on cheque.

Special points – Transport workers very poorly organised.

Publicity – Local bulletins issued.

Defence – Only usual pickets.

Arrests – One member of A.S.L.E.F. and fined £3.

Position on May 12 – General disappointment about the settlement.

Document 25

The Dover dockers
A diary kept by Henry Duckworth, now of Dollingbridge Place, Sussex, deposited in the British Library of Political and Economic Science. Duckworth helped organise the Trinity College, and other, students from Cambridge University who went to Dover docks to keep work going throughout the General Strike.

There I found him telephoning to Dover who appeared delighted at his suggestion and were prepared to receive fifty of us with open arms. . . . A meeting of volunteers was called for 2.30 in my room. . . . By three o'clock the room had been turned into an office, with an office staff of secretaries, . . .
Thursday, May 6th
Birkin, our chauffeur, plus a guard for the return journey, was ordered to be round at Great gate with his 100 m.p.h. Bentley at four o'clock. A.H.S. and I were two minutes late, but by 5.30 we had all posted in and were starting down Trinity Street. . . . Birkin had removed his windscreen in case he should have a brickbat thrown at him in the course of his way back through London. Since he was not actually a member of the so-called 'Dover Fifty'. [They offer their services to the Southern Railway to work on unloading at the Dover Docks.]
Numerous rumours were about as to the strikers' attitude towards us. It was thought that there would be a massed attack on us during the night or an attempt on the part of a single man to get

in and cut the cables of the cranes. The cranes were our most vital spot, upon their being all the work of the day: it would be difficult to exaggerate their importance; it would be impossible to cope with luggage or cargo in the hold of a ship without them. There was only one 'blackleg' who could work them, Fletcher by name: for this reason he had to be taken special care of. He was a pleasant fellow eager to do well so as to get taken on by the SR when the strike was over. He had been dismissed by the Company, so rumour has it – for being mixed up in a theft which took place in the hold of a ship. The party of blackleg labour was made up of all the riff-raff of the town, . . .

Friday, May 7th

Since we had all come down by road there was at our disposal a large number of chauffeurs and their cars, and it seemed a pity not to make use of them. We therefore offered the permanent service of these to the Southern Railway, pleased to be able to repay them in any way possible for the kindness they were showing us. [It was recorded that 97 men attended breakfast that morning but that five had to be sacked or sent back. Later there were one or two minor incidents and some discussion about the pay of these under-graduates, agreed at 1s. 2d. per hour for eight-hour day shifts.]

Sunday, May 9th

. . . Many of the casuals were 'beaten up' coming to the station in the morning and again in the evening when returning from their work owing entirely to inadequate and inefficiently organised police protection.

[There were a few scuffles and the students arranged, by various devices, to get some police protection for them whilst sleeping in the continental expresses in the station, but their period at Dover passed off without major incident. They left Dover on Friday, 14 May and their exploits were later recounted in the June 1926 issue of the *Trinity Magazine*, under the title 'Dover Marine'. It ran as follows.]

A party of eighty, seventy of whom were students, arrived at Dover Station and were organised into gangs.

Document 26

Stand by the miners! An appeal by the Communist Party of Great Britain
Workers' Bulletin, 13 May 1926. Look at the first page of chapter seven for the introduction to this document. . . .

The Right Wing in the General Council bears direct responsibility for throwing away the workers' weapons and leaving them almost defenceless against the capitalists. Throughout the General Strike they deliberately avoided any pledge to fight against wage reductions. They gave prominence to appeals by Archbishops and County Councils to call off the General Strike without guarantee as to living standards. They suppressed the news that scores, sometimes hundreds, of workers were being arrested or batoned for exercising their right of picketing and propaganda. And most of the so-called Left Wing have been no better than the Right. Even now they have not the courage to come openly as a minority in the General Council and join forces with the real majority – the workers – against the united front of Baldwin–Samuel–Thomas.

Document 27

The TUC and the end of the strike
British Worker, 13 May 1926.
'Stand Together'

Fellow Trade Unionists,
The General Strike has ended. It has not failed. It has made possible the resumption of negotiations in the coal industry, and the continuance, during negotiations, of the financial assistance given by the Government. You came out together, in accordance with the instructions of the Executives of your Unions. Return together on their instructions, as and when they are given.

Some employers will approach you as individuals, with the demand that you should accept conditions different from those obtaining before the stoppage began.

Sign no individual agreement. Consult your Union officials and stand by their instructions. Your union will protect you, and will insist that all agreements previously in force shall be maintained intact.

The Trade Union Movement has demonstrated its unity. That unity remains unimpaired. Stick to your Unions.
GENERAL COUNCIL, TRADES UNION CONGRESS

Document 28

The TUC Defends itself.
General Council, *Report to the Conferences of the Executives of Affiliated Unions*, 25 June 1926.

The General Council could not follow the Miners' Executive in the policy of mere negation. Such a course would have been to permit the splendid response of the sympathetic strike to evaporate by a process of attrition, which would have brought the unions to a position of bankruptcy, would have undermined the morale of their membership, and thus have destroyed their capacity to resist attempts that might be made to impose adverse conditions and general discrimination against the active membership when the industries directly engaged in the strike resumed operations.

The Council were satisfied that, however long they continued the strike, they would still be in the same position so far as the attitude of the Miners' Executive was concerned, and consequently the Council was not justified in permitting the unions to continue the sacrifice for another day.

The strike was terminated for one sufficient reason only, namely that in view of the attitude of the Miners' federation its continuance would have rendered its purpose futile.

Document 29

Trade disputes and Trade Union Act, 1927

1. (1) It is hereby declared –
(a) that any strike is illegal if it
    (i)   has any object other than or in addition to the furtherance of a trade dispute or industry in which the strikers are engaged; and
    (ii) is a strike designed to coerce the Government either directly or by inflicting hardship upon the community . . . and it is further declared that it is illegal to commence, or continue, or to apply any sums in furtherance or support of, any such illegal strike. . . .

For the purpose of the foregoing provisions –
(a) a trade dispute shall not be deemed to be within a trade or industry unless it is a dispute between employers and workmen, or between workmen and workmen, in that trade or industry, which is connected with the employment or non-employment or the terms of employment, or with the conditions of labour, of person in that trade or industry; . . .
4. (a) It shall not be lawful to require any member of a trade union to make any contribution to the political fund of a trade union unless he has at some time after the commencement of this Act and before he is first, after the thirty-first day of December, nineteen hundred and twenty-seven, required to make such a contribution

delivered at the head office or some branch office of the trade union, notice in writing in the form set out in the First Schedule to this Act of his willingness to contribute to that fund and has not withdrawn the notice in manner hereinafter; . . .

Document 30

Trade Union membership and rate of unemployment 1920–1939

Year	Membership (000s)	Rate of Change (year/s)	Unemployment (%)	(%)
1920	8,438			7.9
1921	6,633	1920–1	−20.55	16.9
1922	5,625			14.3
1923	5,429			11.7
1924	5,544	1922–5	+2.12	10.3
1925	5,506			11.3
1926	5,219			12.5
1927	4,919			9.7
1928	4,806	1925–8	−12.71	10.8
1929	4,858			10.4
1930	4,842			16.1
1931	4,614			21.3
1932	4,444			22.1
1933	4,392	1929–33	−9.59	21.3
1934	4,590	1933–9	+43.39	16.7
1939	6,298			10.5

Many sources

Document 31

Workers Directly and Indirectly Involved in Disputes and the Number of Days Lost, 1920–1939

Year	Workers (000s)	Days Lost (000s)	Year (000s)	Workers (000s)	Days Lost
1920	1,932	26,568	1930	307	4,339
1921	1,801	85,872	1931	490	6,908
1922	552	19,850	1932	379	6,448
1923	405	10,672	1933	136	1,072
1924	613	8,424	1934	134	959
1925	441	7,952	1935	271	1,955
1926	2,750	162,233	1936	316	1,829
1927	108	1,174	1937	597	3,413
1928	124	1,388	1938	274	1,334
1929	533	8,287	1939	337	1,356

Document 32

Unemployment figures for insured workers

Date	Total (000s)	Date	Total (000s)
December 1920	691	December 1929	1,334
March 1921	1,355	December 1930	2,500
June 1921	2,171	December 1931	2,500
December 1921	2,038	January 1932	2,850
December 1922	1,464	January 1933	2,950
December 1923	1,229	January 1934	2,400
December 1924	1,263	January 1935	2,290
December 1925	1,243	January 1936	2,130
December 1926	1,432	January 1937	1,670
December 1927	1,194	January 1938	1,810

Variety of sources, including K. Laybourn, *Britain on the Breadline: A Social and Political History of Britain between the Wars*, Sutton, Stroud, 1990, p. 8.

Document 33

Money rates and cost-of-living index, 1919–1930

(1914 = 100)						
Year	1919	1920	1921	1922	1923	1924
Cost-of-living Index	215	249	226	183	174	175
Money wage rates	215–20	270–80	210	170	165	170
Year	1925	1926	1927	1928	1929	1930
Cost-of-living Index	176	172	168	166	164	158
Money Wage rates	175	175	170	170	170	170

Based upon *Statistical Abstract of UK, 1930*, p 115

Document 34

Real incomes, real wages, wages rates and earnings, prices, 1924–1938

(1924 = 100)	*1924*	*1929*	*1931*	*1932*	*1934*	*1935*	*1938*
Wage rates	100	96		90	90	90.5	99.5
Earnings	100	98		89	93	97	103
Prices	100	82	62.5	61	63	64	73
Real Income per head *(with unemp.)*	100	111.8	103.7		115.5	120.9	
Real Income *per head* *(ex. unemp.)*	100	108.3	110		116.4	120.7	
Real Wages	100	104	114	116.5	115.5		

A. L. Bowley, *Studies in National Income*, pp. 62–3, and other sources.)

Document 35

General indicators

Year	Union membership (000s)	Union density (%)	Stoppages (1914 = 100)	Cost of living (July 1914 = 100)	Weekly wage rates
1914	4,117	24.7	972	100	100
1918	6,461	38.1	1,165	203	195–200
1919	7,837	46.0	1,352	215	215–220
1920	8,253	48.2	1,607	249	270–280
1921	6,512	37.9	763	226	231
1922	5,573	32.1	576	183	191
1923	5,382	30.7	628	174	188
1924	5,463	30.9	710	175	194
1925	5,430	30.4	603	176	196
1926	5,152	28.6	323	172	195
1927	4,860	26.8	308	167.5	196
1928	4,753	25.9	302	166	194
1929	4,804	26.0	431	164	193
1930	4,783	25.7	422	158	191
1931	4,569	24.3	420	147.5	189
1932	4,395	22.9	357	140	183

Based on Clegg, *British Trade Unions II*, p. 569.)

Document 36

Union Membership

	1921	1925	% change	1926	1928	% change
Coal Mining	936,653	885,789	−5.44	762,916	592,379	− 6.31
Paper and Printing	201,614	207,151	+2.75	185,975	180,878	−12.68
Railways	560,875	528,764	−4.32	491,861	412,037	−22.08
Transport and general	1,086,783	919,172	−15.42	860,485	769,483	−16.29
Building	460,998	334,528	−27.43	328,970	308,697	− 7.72
Textiles	730,895	626,973	−14.22	620,105	591,620	− 5.64
Eng. and Shipbuild.	895,043	594,568	−33.57	573,083	540,805	− 9.04
Iron and Steel	131,661	86,811	−33.99	83,851	66,498	− 3.49

	1932	% change 1928–32	1939	% change 1932–9
Coal Mining	554,015	−6.31	707,012	+ 28.05
Paper and Printing	184,218	+1.85	224,188	+ 21.69
Railways	399,184	−3.14	470,033	+ 17.75
Transport and general lab.	660,180	−22.0	1,218,911	+ 84.64
Building	247,752	−11.0	Building. and furnit,	+27.89
Textiles	492,473	−16.76	419,559	−14.81
Eng. and shipbuilding	472,251	−12.58	Total for eng.	
Iron and Steel	53,983	−18.82	ship. and Iron	
		and Steel	936,125	+ 77.89

Based on *Abstract of Labour Statistics*, vol. 21, 1933 and *Ministry of Labour Gazette*, October 1940, and quoted in Phillips, *General Strike*, p. 283.

Bibliographical Essay

All the sources on the General Strike, both primary and secondary, are referred to in the footnotes throughout the book. The main purpose of this section is to indicate the main books and articles which might be consulted profitably on the various issues raised by the General Strike. It is by no means exhaustive.

In the early and mid-1970s there was almost a surfeit of books dealing with the General Strike. The best of these is probably G.A. Phillips, *The General Strike: The Politics of Industrial Conflict*, London, 1976, whose main interest was to examine the trade union perspective on the dispute although it also attempted to survey all the major events. Among the others is M. Morris, *The General Strike, 1926*, London, 1976, which covers all aspects of the strike in detail and which particularly focuses upon the events. Indeed, it is the only major book on the General Strike which is still being published. P. Renshaw, *The General Strike*, London, 1975 also attempts to provide a full review of all the aspects of the dispute. Other books that focus generally on the dispute include C. Farman, *The General Strike, May 1926*, London, 1972 and, from an earlier era, J. Symons, *The General Strike*, London, 1957. There is also the 'Our History' Communist Party interpretation of the causes, events and consequences of the strike in J. Skelley, editor, *The General Strike, 1926*, London, 1976.

Some libraries still contain copies of earlier books produced in the wake of the dispute. The best, without a doubt, is that by W. H. Crook, *The General Strike: A Study of Labor's Tragic Weapon in*

154

Theory and Practice, North Carolina, 1931 which forms the basis of many later works. For a more partial view R. P. Arnot, *The General Strike. May, 1926: Its Origins and History*, London, 1926 and H. Fyfe, *Behind the Scenes of the Great Strike*, London, 1926 are about the best, although R. P. Dutt, *The Meaning of the General Strike*, London, 1926 provides a useful analysis from the Communist point of view. However, if it can be obtained, E. Burns, *The General Strike, May 1926; Trades Councils in Action*, London, 1926, provides an excellent survey of how the councils of action were organised and how effective they were.

There are several autobiographies and biographies which add greatly to our knowledge of the dispute. Of the autobiographies Lord Citrine's, *Men and Work*, London, 1964, is the most revealing and includes his diary of the Nine Days but others, such as A. Horner, *Incorrigible Rebel*, London, 1960, and Will Paynter, *My Generation*, London, 1972, are also useful. Yet there are many important biographies which are far less self-conscious. See especially, P. Davies, *A. J. Cook*, Manchester, 1987; A. Bullock, *The Life and Times of Ernest Bevin I, Trade Union Leader 1881–1940*, London, 1960; R. K. Middlemass and J. Barnes, *Baldwin: A Biography*, London, 1969. H. Montgomery Hyde, *Baldwin: The Unexpected Prime Minister*, London, 1973; Lord Birkenhead, *F. E. – the life of F. E. Smith*, London, 1960. Jack Lawson's work on Herbert Smith, entitled, *The Man in the Cap*, London, 1941 provides a sympathetic study of Smith and G. Blaxland, *A Life of Unity*, London, 1964, is rather too kind to Jimmy Thomas.

The literature on the coal industry is extensive. R. P. Arnot, *The Miners' Years of Struggle: A History of the Miners' Federation of Great Britain (from 1910 onwards)*, London, 1953 is excellent from the point of view of the miners and, for a whole survey of the industry, from 1913 to 1946, there is B. Supple, *The History of the British Coal Industry, Vol. 4: The Political Economy of Decline*, Oxford, 1987.

There are many local studies of the dispute, mostly in article form. Amongst the best, and most easily accessible, are A. Mason, *The General Strike in the North East*, Hull, 1970; R. I. Hills, *The General Strike in York, 1926*, York, 1980; T. Woodhouse, 'The General Strike in Leeds', *Northern History*, 1982 and J. H. Porter, 'Devon and the General Strike, 1926', *International Review of Social History*, 1978.

The attitude of employers has been of crucial concern in recent years and in this respect two main articles might be consulted. They are C. Wrigley, 'Trade Unionists, Employers and the Cause of Industrial Unity and Peace, 1916–1921' in C. Wrigley and J. Shepherd, editor, *On the Move: Essays in Labour* and Transport History presented to Philip Bagwell, London, 1991; and A. McIvor, 'Essay in Anti-Labour History', *Society for the Study of Labour History, Bulletin*, 1988. The attitude of the Government has been admirably put by R. Lowe in 'Government and Industrial Relations, 1919–1939', in C. J. Wrigley, editor, *A History of British Industrial Relations, II*, Brighton, 1981.

The role of the Communist Party, already alluded to, can be studied in L. J. Macfarlane, *The British Communist Party: Its Origins and Development until 1929*, London, 1966 and J. Klugmann, *The History of the Communist Party, vol. II*, London, 1969. R. Martin, *Communism and British Trade Unions 1924–1933*, Oxford, 1969 is a useful study of the National Minority Movement which touched upon its role in the General Strike.

Finally, there are many more general histories of trade unions and industrial relations which deal with the 1920s. The following are some of the most useful: C. J. Wrigley, *A History of British Industrial Relations II*, Brighton, 1987; H. A. Clegg, *A History of British Trade Unions since 1889, Vol. II 1911–33*, Oxford, 1985; and K. Laybourn, *A History of British Trade Unionism c 1770–1990*, Stroud, 1992. For documents on the General Strike look at K. Laybourn, editor, *British Trade Unionism v 1770–1990: A Reader in History*, Stroud, 1991.

Index

Arnot, Robin Page, 3, 12, 61, 123, 125–6, 155
Astbury Judgement, 80, 107

Baldwin, Stanley, 3–4, 14–15, 29 30, 39 42, 44, 54, 58, 80, 84, 89, 96, 106, 110, 119, 133–5, 139–40, 147
Barber, Walter, 52, 64–5
Barnsley, 91
BBC, 80, 133–4
Beveridge, W. H., 36
Bevin, Ernest, 19, 21, 35–6, 44, 45, 49, 51, 84, 86, 96, 101–2, 109, 115, 118, 121
Birkenhead formula, 43
Birkenhead, Lord, 42
Birmingham, 63, 68, 71, 90–1, 93, 115
   Trades Council, 59
'Black Friday', 13, 17, 19, 27, 45
Bolton Council of Action, 60, 63, 142
Bondfield, Margaret, 51
Bradford, 33, 59, 71, 90, 114
   Council of Action, 64, 66
   Dyers, 65

Dyers' Association, 65
General Strike, 63–6
Independent Labour Party, 65
Labour Party, 65
Pioneer, 90
Strike Bulletin, 71
Trades Council, 64
Worker, 64, 134
Brighton, 91
Bulletin, 60
Bristol, 33
British Gazette, 56, 58, 79–80
British Worker, 53, 70, 80–1, 143–4, 147
Bromley, John, 29, 39, 105
Bullock, Alan, 5, 86, 101–3, 155
Burns, Emile, 4, 49, 59, 61–2, 141–5, 155
busmen, 93–4

Chamberlain, Neville, 93
Cheltenham, 91
Churchill, Winston, 14, 30–2, 56, 79, 96, 130–1
Citrine, Walter (*later* Lord), 1, 5–6, 28–9, 32, 34–5, 39, 42, 44–5, 82–4, 89, 108, 112, 118, 129,

137, 139, 155
Civil Constabulary Reserve, 57
Clegg, Hugh A., 6, 14, 102–3, 112,
    152, 156
Clinton, Alan, 59–60
Clynes, J. R., 11
coal dispute (1925), 23
coal industry, 36
coal subsidy, 31
Communist Party of Great Britain,
    3, 5, 12–13, 24, 50, 72–3, 78,
    114, 126–7, 146–7
communists, 8, 70–3, 114
Cook, A. J., 5, 10–12, 32, 34–5,
    37–9, 44, 49, 78, 82, 95–6, 100,
    104, 134
    The Nine Days, 45, 96, 100, 104
Co-operative Union and societies,
    53, 142–5
Coventry Council of Action, 143–4
    Labour Monthly, 143
Crook, W. H., 9, 86, 154–5

Daily Herald, 53
Daily Mail, 43–5, 134
Davies, Paul, 11, 95, 155
Davison, Lily, 61–2
Devon, 66
disputes, 12
Doncaster, 91
Dorking, 144
'Dover Dockers' *or* 'Dover Fifty',
    55–6, 145–6
Duckworth, Henry, 55–6, 145–6
Dutt, R. J., 155

earnings, 151
Economic League, 33–4
Emergency Powers Act (1920), 16,
    122
employers 110–11
Engineering and Allied
    Employers' Federation, 93

Farman, C., 57, 78, 154
Feather, Vic, 71
Foster, John, 15
Fife, Hamilton, 53, 155

General and Municipal Workers'
    Union, 63, 91
General Union of Textile Workers,
    17
Glasgow, 91
Gloucester, 63
    dockers, 91
Government objectives, 54–8, 110,
    130
Great Western Railway, 66

Hayday, Arthur, 29
Henderson, Arthur, 11, 41, 44
Hendon Trades Council and Joint
    Strike Committee, 144
Hicks, George, 29, 31, 112–13
Hirst, W., 65
Holton, Bob, 10
Huddersfield, 69
Hull, 70, 90

Industrial Alliance, 21, 35, 125–6

Jacques, Martin, 103, 108–9
Joynson-Hicks, William, 30, 32–3

Labour Party, 104, 106, 114–15
Labour Research Department, 59,
    61, 142
Lane, Tony, 12
Laraman, G. H., 52
Lee, Kenneth, 36
Leeds, 91
    and District Joint Trade Union
        Committee, 63
    communist march, 70
    strike organisations, 62, 66

Index

Trades Council, and Council of Action, 63, 144
Weekly Citizen, 144
Worker's Defence Corps, 70
Liverpool, 33, 68, 92
Council of Action, 141-1
Lloyd George, David, 16–18, 32, 79–80

McDonald, G. W., 110–11
MacDonald, J. Ramsay, 32, 35, 41, 44, 80, 114–15, 132
McIvor, Arthur, 33–4
Macmillan, H. P., 29–30
Macmillan Inquiry Report, 29–30
Manchester, 69
Guardian, 94
Trades and Labour Council, 131
Mann, Tom, 10–11
Marchbank, J., 29
Mason, Tony, 57, 62, 91, 155
Mellor, W., 131
Merseyside, 66, 141
Council of Action, 61, 92
Methel Workers' Defence Corps, 70
Middlesbrough, 70
Council of Action, 60, 62
mine owners, 96
miners, 18–19, 79–87 *passim*, 94–7, 105, 133, 135–6
lock-out (1926), 9, 95–7
Miners' Federation of Great Britain, 10, 12, 18, 20–1, 35, 37–40, 84, 95–7, 104–5, 148
Mining Association, 38, 40, 81, 96, 127
Mining Industry Act (1926), 96
Ministry of Health
circular 636, 33
circular 703, 54, 131–2
Ministry of Transport, 33
Mond, Sir Alfred, 111, 113

Mond-Turner talks, 108, 113–14
Morris, Margaret, 4, 13, 71, 90, 154
Mosley, Oswald, 90

National Association of Unions in the Textile Trade, 22
National Government, 115
National Minority Movement, 63, 72, 114, 156
National Trade Union Defence Committee, 108
National Transport Committee, 52
National Transport Workers' Federation, 19
National Union of Railwaymen, 19–20, 42, 52–3, 66–7, 69, 141
National Union of Textile Workers, 22
Newcastle Strike Committee, 61
Trades Council, 52
Newport, 91
Northumberland and Durham General Council Joint Committee, 61
Nottingham, 63, 93, 96

Organisation of the Maintenance of Supplies, 33, 55, 63, 68, 123–4, 126–7

permits, 52, 59, 64
Perth Strike Committee, 145
Phillips, Gordon, 4, 6, 13, 29, 31, 39, 46, 57, 78, 86, 90, 102–3, 115–16, 153, 154
Pickles, Alderman A., 65
Plebs League, 67
Plymouth, 66, 68
football match, 66
tram riot, 66, 70
policing, 69–72
Porter, J. H., 66, 155
Postgate, Raymond, 62

Poulton, E. L., 29
prices, 151
Pugh, Arthur, 39–42, 44, 83–5,
    105, 129, 136, 139

railway accidents, 69
railway companies, 69, 93
railway men, 67, 94
real incomes, 151
real wages, 151
'Red Friday', 2, 27–32, 107, 123,
    127
Renshaw, Patrick, 4–5, 13, 31, 78,
    90, 102–3, 154

Samuel, Sir Herbert, 5, 79, 81–3,
    85, 89, 105, 120, 134, 136–9,
    147
    Commission (*Report of the Royal
    Commission on the Coal Industry*
    (1925/6)), 27, 36–9, 42, 45, 54,
    82, 95–6, 110, 118–19, 127–8,
    138
    Memorandum, 5, 82–6, 89,
    105–6, 119, 136–8
Sankey Commission, 16, 18, 28,
    46, 79
Sheffield Central Dispute
    Committee, 90
    Council of Action, 62
Sheps, A., 86
Shipley, 64
    communists, 64, 70
Simon, Sir John, 80
Skelley, J., 154
Smith, Herbert, 31, 37, 39, 44, 95
Snowden, Philip, 115
St. Albans Council of Action, 62
Steel-Maitland, Sir Arthur, 22, 42,
    85, 95–6, 110
strike days lost, 108– 110–11,
    149–50
Strike News, 60

Swales, A. J., 29–30, 42, 44
Symons, Julian, 31, 57, 71, 86, 154
syndicalism, 10–11, 103

Teeside Federation, 61
The Miners' Next Step, 10
The Mining Situation, 40–1
The Northern Light, 60
Thomas, J. H., 19, 32, 35, 41–2, 61,
    67, 78–9, 81, 83, 114–15, 118,
    147
Tillett, Ben, 29, 120
Tracey, Herbert, 32
Trades Dispute Act (1906), 11
Trades Dispute Act (1927), 65, 80,
    106–7, 110–11, 115, 121
Trades Union Congress, 2, 4–6, 9,
    13, 24, 28, 37–40, 42, 45–6,
    52–5, 57–8, 61, 78–86, 89, 94,
    101, 103–9, 111, 113–15, 118,
    124–5, 128–30, 132, 134–5, 138,
    141, 147
    'Black Circular', 114
    General Council, 1–2, 5, 12, 21,
    27–30, 34–5, 39–43, 45, 50–4,
    60, 78–87, 88, 90, 96–7, 100–1,
    103–9, 113–15, 119–20, 122,
    124–5, 128–30, 134–5, 139, 141,
    147
    Joint Consultative Committee,
    20
    Negotiating Committee, 5, 41,
    43, 81–3, 86, 119
    Powers and Orders Committee,
    51
    Publicity Committee, 51
    Special Industrial Committee,
    29–30, 35, 38–9, 41
    Strike Organisation Committee,
    51
    Ways and Means Committee, 51
trade union funds, 108
trade union membership, 103, 108,

111–12, 149, 153
Transport and General Workers'
    Union, 21, 93
Triple Alliance, 10, 17, 19
Turner, Ben, 17, 23

unemployment figures, 150

wage rates, 151
Wakefield, 90
Walkden, A. G., 29
Webb, Beatrice, 101–2
Westminster Worker, 60
Williams, A. R., 91

Wilson, Horace, 42, 84
Wolverhampton Council of Action, 60
Workers' Bulletin, 73
Workers' Chronicle, 52, 60
Workers' Weekly, 73
Woodhouse, Tom, 62–3, 155
wool and worsted textile dispute
    and lock-out (1925), 1, 22–4,
    110, 123
Wrigley, Chris, 11, 18, 102, 109,
    156

York, 68, 91–3
    strike organisation, 66